You're Sittin' on Boomey!

The Best of Ludlow Porch

LUDLOW PORCH

LONGSTREET PRESS
Atlanta, GA

Published by
LONGSTREET PRESS, INC.
2140 Newmarket Parkway
Suite 122
Marietta, Georgia 30067

Printed in the United States of America

1st printing, 1997

Library of Congress Catalog Number 97-71929

ISBN 1-56352-436-8

Electronic film prep by OGI, FOREST PARK, GA

Jacket design by Audrey Graham

for Nancy
my hand-holding sweetheart

FOREWORD

I'm not sure exactly how old I was when I first met Boomey. I would guess about three and a half. He was the best friend I ever had.

Boomey always smiled. He played whatever I wanted to play, and he never argued with me about who got to play with which toy. When friends of the family came to visit, I would hear them ask my mother, "Who is Luddie talking to?" My mother would say, "He's talking to his imaginary friend, Boomey." The visitor would always say in a voice dripping with sugar, "Isn't that sweet?" What they were really thinking was, "That little boy must have the IQ of a lemon."

The only reason that didn't bother me was that I didn't know what imaginary meant.

It was a long time before I realized that I was the only one who could see Boomey. The grown-ups all pretended to see him. They would say things like, "Well, how is old Boomey today?" I would say, "He is fine." They were afraid that if I found out Boomey was not real it would blow the whole Santa Claus, Tooth Fairy, Easter Bunny thing.

I didn't realize it at the time, of course, but looking back on it, Boomey had a great influence on my life. He taught me that it was possible for two children to play for hours without conflict; he taught me that smiling was good (Boomey never stopped smiling).

One day I was in our parlor with Boomey. We were sitting on the sofa when there was a knock on the front door. I opened the door and it was our preacher from the Presbyterian church. He asked to see my grandmother. I told him to come in and have a seat. He walked right to the sofa and sat down on top of poor Boomey.

I could not believe my eyes. This very large Presbyterian was on top of Boomey! I ran right up to him screaming, "You're sittin' on Boomey! You're killing Boomey," tears flowing, arms flailing. I knew that under that man was my dead friend. My grandmother came running into the room. There I was, standing in front of the preacher screaming, "You're sittin' on Boomey!" at the top of my lungs.

Without missing a beat, my grandmother shouted, "Get up, get up, Preacher. Hurry! You're sitting on Boomey!"

He jumped to his feet, eyes as big as two hubcaps, saying over and over, "I'm sorry. I'm sorry. What did I do wrong?"

I don't remember how this story ended, but I do remember that the only calm person there was Boomey.

One day Boomey stopped coming to my house. When I asked my mother where he was, she said that imaginary friends don't stay around forever. I said someday, he'll be back. I was wrong. Boomey never came back.

Growing up is hard.

CONTENTS

A View From the Porch — 1

The Cornbread Chronicles — 27

There's Nothing Neat About Seeing Your Feet — 49

Can I Just Do It Til I Need Glasses? — 69

Weirdos, Winos & Defrocked Priests — 77

Who Cares About Apathy? — 97

Jonas Wilkerson Was a Gravy-Suckin' Pig — 113

Honest, Officer, The Midget Was on Fire When I Got Here — 117

Lewis & Me & Skipper Makes 3 — 135

Beating a Dead Horse Is More Fun Than You Think — 151

We're All In This Alone — 169

A VIEW FROM THE PORCH (1981)

OCCUPATIONAL HAZARDS

Mandrake Was Not from Around Here

I don't guess a day goes by that somebody doesn't tell me a sure-fire way to lose weight. I wouldn't mind so much, but the people who talk to me about it usually weigh about eighty pounds and have never had a weight problem. Let the record clearly show, fun-seekers, that I know how to lose weight. I don't know how to keep it off, but I know how to lose it.

In my life I have lost over two thousand pounds. Think about that. Over two thousand pounds. That's the equivalent of a large horse.

I think now you probably understand why I resent some emaciated little runt telling me how to lose weight. Dear Lord, how I detest skinny people! Not only have I tried every diet introduced in this country over the last thirty years, but I have also invented a few that nobody ever heard of. I invented the famous elephant diet. You can have one elephant a week, cooked any way you want it. The only thing is, you have to catch it yourself and kill it with a butter knife.

I guess the wildest thing I ever tried was a hypnotist. A friend of mine knew about a hypnotist named Mandrake Wilson. My friend assured me that Mandrake could put me under and when I woke up, I'd be all set to give up food.

I decided I'd give Mandrake a try. He was wearing a great velvet turban, a black cape and no shoes. And, oh yeah! He had a ring on his great toe. I knew one thing right away about Mandrake: he was not from around here.

He laid me down on a roll-away bed, turned the lights down low, put a Lefty Frizell record on and started to talk to me real soft and slow. Kinda like Clark Gable used to talk to Claudette Colbert. He told me that when he snapped his fingers I would wake up and not be hungry.

He snapped his fingers and I woke up and ate his medallion. It cost me seven-fifty to find out that medallions give me heartburn.

Where's the Service in Service Station?

Whatever happened to the idea that the customer is always right? Now, I know that is a cliché from the past, but a lot of good businesses were built on the customer being right. In case you hadn't noticed it, that's as gone with the wind as Tara is.

Do you remember going into a gas station and the attendant bounding out, smiling and saying, "Can I hep you?" And before you could get out of the service station, he had checked your oil, tires and battery, washed your windshield, and offered to baby-sit for you on Saturday night.

The first thing you see when you go into a gas station now is a sign that says "due to a shortage of computer parts, the amount shown on the pump represents one-half of your actual purchase." Now, just think about that. There ain't no such thing as a shortage of computer parts. They're just too cheap to buy new pumps, so they let you do their math for them.

The next sign you see is one on the door that says they accept exact amount only. Now think about that for a moment. Exact Amount Only. Now, they want your business, or they wouldn't put their silly commercials on TV. But they only want your business if they don't have to make change or tell you how much the pump says you owe.

Then you go inside to pay. Whatever happened to the smiling attendant? Well, he's still there; he just doesn't go outside any more. Gone forever are the coveralls with his name over the pocket; gone forever is the comment "Looks like you're a quart low." Gone forever is the clean windshield and the checked transmission fluid.

But you know what I think bothers me the most? I feel that it's basically un-American to pay a gas station attendant who has clean hands.

Dr. Kildare Never Wore Bell-Bottoms

I can stand anything but pain, because I found out years ago that pain hurts. As a matter of fact, the more pain you have, the more it hurts.

The story I'm about to tell you is true; only the names have been changed to prevent a punch in the mouth.

One day I was walking out my back door and tripped and fell down about four steps. I tried to break the fall with my hands out in front of me and really hurt both my wrists. I was in such pain that I was just sure that my chubby little wrists were broken.

I called my doctor's office and his nurse told me that my family doctor was in the hospital. It seems that he had suffered a heart attack while water-skiing. I'll never forgive him for not being available in my hour of need. He's a real nice old boy, but bad to have random heart attacks. I've been telling him for years that he needs to see a good doctor.

Well, to make a long story short — if it isn't too late — I didn't know what to do, so I called a friend and she said she had a great doctor, and she would call him and see if he could see me.

I went to visit this wonderful healer of the wrists. I was really in pain by the time I got to his office.

I told the receptionist I was there, and she told me to have a seat in the waiting room. Sitting there, I noticed about four hundred pictures on the walls, all of this doctor, taken in Vietnam. In the pictures he was treating little children and wearing this big .45 automatic on his hip.

Now, when I tell you there were four hundred pictures on the wall, that's no exaggeration. I knew that I was in the office of an egomaniac.

About the time I was getting ready to leave, the receptionist said, "The doctor will see you now."

I was led into a little examining room and told to sit down. I had been there about two minutes when the biggest, ugliest nurse this side of Villa Rica came in with a clipboard and said, "We need to check your weight, Mr. Porch."

I said, "I hope you're just gonna weigh my wrists, because that's all that hurts."

She didn't think it was very funny. She finished weighing me, then she took my temperature, then she checked my blood pressure. Every time she would check something, she would write the results on a clipboard that said ATLANTIC ICE AND COAL on the back of it.

I tell you, fun-seekers, before that nurse finished with me she had checked everything but my class ring.

As she was leaving the room she said, "The doctor will be with you in a minute."

"Could you get me something for the pain?" I asked. "I'm really hurting."

She said, "You can't have anything till after the doctor sees you. Would you like some water?"

I said, "I'm not dirty, lady. I'm in pain!"

She didn't even smile as she closed the door.

Well, about ten minutes went by, and I was fit to be tied.

Suddenly the great healer came into the room. He had his nurse's clipboard with him … you know, the one that said ATLANTIC ICE AND COAL on the back.

I tell you, this doctor was something to behold. He was about five feet tall, and was wearing white bell-bottom pants with a flowered Hawaiian shirt and blue tennis shoes.

He came into the room reading his clipboard and never even looked up.

He said, "Mr. Porch, you are fat."

And I said, "Yes, doctor, and you are short. Now, I can leave here and lose weight, but what are you going to do?"

I knew from this moment on that any chance for a good relationship with this doctor was shot to hell. So I left and got myself two Ace bandages and some Bufferin. Then I sacrificed two chickens to the Moon God.

A Ride with the Cisco Kid

About two years ago, I had to go to New York City on business. Now, New York is a right nice place to visit, but when you are there on business and are in a hurry, the traffic and hustle and bustle can soon get on your nerves.

The folks up there are all in a hurry, and you get the impression that you'd better not interrupt their organized mayhem, because most of them are kind of quarrelsome and would not mind hurting your feelings.

They talk funny, and ain't none of them from around here.

I could feel the hostility as I got off the airplane. I got my luggage and went outside to get a cab. I got in line just in time to see the taxi dispatcher and a customer get in a fist fight about how much the fare should be to Brooklyn. It wasn't a bad fight, but neither one of them could stand a chance against a red-headed south Georgia waitress I know named Roberta.

Well, it finally came my turn and I got in a taxi.

The driver never turned around. I said, "Do you know where 500 Park Avenue is?"

He said, "Jes."

I said, "Sure is a nice day."

He said, "Jes."

I said, "How do you think the Mets will do this year?"

He said, "Jes."

There was a big sign in the taxi that said "Driver will

not change any bill larger than $5." The smallest I had was a twenty. I thought, "Here I am nine hundred miles from the nearest glass of buttermilk, stuck in a taxi with the Cisco Kid, and not only can he not change a twenty, but I'm not gonna be able to explain to him that a twenty is the smallest bill I have."

I guess the Lord looks after you when you are north of Richmond, because about that time we came to a tollbooth. I said, "I'll pay this."

I rolled the window down and handed the toll booth operator my twenty. He made an ugly face and said, "Is that the smallest bill you got, fella?"

I could see the anger in his face. I said, "Jes."

He said, "I hate people who give me big bills."

I said, "Jes."

He took the bill and said something insulting about Puerto Ricans and threw my change in the window.

As we pulled away, I yelled, "How's your mama 'n' 'em?"

If you can't join them, beat them.

Never Trust a Man in a Tall White Hat

I don't particularly like chefs. No, that's not right. It would be more accurate to say that I dislike some chefs. Well, that's not right, either. I guess the fact of the matter is, I hate all chefs.

Now, let me say real quick that I don't dislike cooks. But when cooks stop being cooks and turn into chefs, they become my mortal enemy, because the first thing they do is start to act real stuck-up. They put on a snow-white uniform and a tall, silly hat that makes them look like a cross between a polar bear and a Ku Klux Klanner. Then they have to change their names. Leon becomes Heinrich and Bubba becomes Pierre. Then they decide that they know how you should like your steaks.

Now, let me say that I like my steaks well done. It's not that I mind the sight of raw meat, but a well-done steak tastes better to me. Eating a rare steak is to me a lot like chewing Dubble Bubble gum.

I'll never forget the time I was in a real fancy place in Birmingham, Alabama. I told the waiter I wanted my steak well done.

He said, "Chef Ramon is not going to like that."

I said, "Well, Chef Ramon ain't going to eat it, and I'm not either if it ain't well done. And not only that — I don't want nothing on my baked potato but a dob of cow butter."

The waiter walked away muttering something about me being an uncouth barbarian.

Well, you probably guessed the end of the story. My steak came back burned to a crisp. I ate it and didn't say a word.

When the waiter brought my bill, I wrote him a check for the price of the meal, and as I left, I heard the waiter say to the cashier, "Wait 'til he tries to digest that steak."

I turned around and said, "Wait until you try to cash that check."

I'm sure looking forward to the day when microwave ovens make all chefs obsolete.

THE STATE OF THE NATION

An Open Letter to My Favorite Uncle

Dear Uncle Sam,

Well, I know you haven't heard from me in quite some time, so I thought I would drop you a line.

I know you have been just catching fits the last few years, and I just felt like you would like to know that a lot of your nieces and nephews out here still love you. As a matter of fact, Unk, you have always been richly blessed with relatives who not only love you but are willing to go to bat for you anytime you need help.

I guess this family pride started back a couple of hundred years ago, when a relative of yours named Patrick Henry stood up in a Richmond church, shook his fist at his in-laws in Europe, and said, "I know not what course others may take, but as for me, give me liberty or give me death!" And don't forget your nephew Stephen Decatur, who said he was with you, right or wrong.

Oh, yes, Unk. Your folks have always been there, from Bunker Hill to Bella Woods; from Mt. Suribachi to the Chosen Reservoir.

But, Unk, in the last few years some strange things have happened. Folks have pushed you around some, and you have been the soul of patience. Why, they even kidnapped fifty-two of your nieces and nephews. Frankly, Unk, it looks like they have mistaken your goodness for weakness.

Unk, I think it's time you squared away the cock-
roach countries of the world. Let them know, Unk,
we're with you and let them know that anytime, anywhere in the world gangsters and kidnappers want to
kick sand in your face, there'll be hell to pay.

Tell them, Unk, that an American embassy is part of
this great country, and the next one that is attacked,
you're gonna roll up those red-white-and-blue sleeves
and make 'em sorry they ever saw the light of day. And
Unk, in the name of God, don't let them burn another
American flag. No. Not one more.

I guess what I'm trying to say, Unk, is: Do what you
have to do to make us proud again, 'cause we're with
you and we love you.

Your Nephew,
Ludlow

Meteorology Complicates My Life

I think it was Mark Twain who first said, "Everybody talks about the weather but nobody does anything about it." I guess that's been true since Adam and Eve tried to call Don Hastings to find out how to prune an apple tree.

Any time there is a lull or a dead spot in the conversation, you can count on somebody saying, "Sure is a nice day," or "Mighty cold for this time of the year," or they throw in, "Do you think it's ever going to rain?"

Nope. Still can't do anything about the weather, but boy, how we love to talk about it! Until TV came along, we limited our weather talk to a few of these well-worn phrases, but then one day about the time *I Love Lucy* and *You Bet Your Life* were becoming household words, somebody got the idea that there was a buck to be made doing weather reports on TV. Now, the longer it goes on, the more profitable it becomes and the sillier it gets. Now they make a simple weather forecast a production to rival a Busby Berkeley musical.

The TV moguls decided early on that it wasn't good enough to have weathermen. No, sir, they went out and hired meteorologists. Until Johnny Beckman came along, I thought a high was something you got at cocktail parties.

Have you ever thought of how much trouble TV goes to to tell you that it may rain tomorrow, but it probably won't? They've got satellites floating around in outer space sending us back pictures of the weather.

What ever happened to your Uncle Fred's corn that hurt when it was going to rain?

And just plain old regular-issue radar wasn't good enough for them. They had to have Color Radar. I can hardly stand it.

You know what I want to hear just one more time before I die? I want to hear one old-timer say to another old-timer, "Looks like a bad cloud acomin' up down Jacks Creek."

And the other old man says, "Yep, when a cloud comes up down Jacks Creek, it's gonna be a frog-strangler."

Stick that in your TV barometer and see who will chart it!

What Good Old Days?

Do you remember just a few short years back, when there were no interstate highways, and when you started to drive from Atlanta to Florida, you knew that you were eight hard hours away from the Florida line? The roads in south Georgia had pot holes that you could lose a Boy Scout troop in. Every barn had "See Rock City" painted on its roof, mules and cows ran loose, and you had to be careful or you'd wind up with a grill full of mule.

Now, it was a hard trip, but I personally feel that it was more fun to travel in those days. The new highways are nice, and nobody is going to argue that they are not safer. But sometimes don't you long for the old days of travel? Take the signs, for example. When was the last time you saw a Burma Shave sign? You sure can't have Burma Shave signs on the interstate, because you drive by so fast, you couldn't tell what the heck they said. Sometimes don't you just yearn to return to the thrilling days of yesteryear when you saw the first little red sign and then watched the jingle unfold? Jingles like:

What you shouted
May be true
But did you hear
What he called you?
Burma Shave.

Or how about the places where you used to eat? Eating on the road was an adventure in those days. You never knew if you were going to get a gourmet meal or if you were going to be poisoned.

And don't forget the souvenir stores, where you could buy anything from a live, baby alligator to a fire-cracker big enough to blow up Tyler, Texas.

And let's not forget about the south Georgia police officers who protected the natives from the speeding tourist. These folks really enjoyed their work. If they caught you going one mile over the speed limit, they would pull you over and give you their classic line.

They'd walk up to the car and say, "Let me see your drime liam."

And then no matter what your license said, or what you said, you got a ticket. But they made it mighty con-venient for you; you were allowed to pay your fine right there on the side of the road. Doesn't it make you won-der why we call the good old days "the good old days"?

They're About to Go Too Far

A recent news story off the wire said that a three-year study in Europe has concluded that fish can feel pain just like animals do. As a result of that finding, Britain's Royal Society for the Prevention of Cruelty to Animals says it may push for outlawing the use of hooks in fishing. Some members of the society argue that the only humane way to catch a fish is with a net.

I don't know for sure if this movement will ever catch on in Great Britain, but I can assure you of one thing: it's almost certain to get some backers in the United States.

Now, the reason I know that is because we just love to pull for the underdog in this country and, after all, who is a bigger underdog than a fish?

You remember the movie *Jaws*, with that poor, old shark being annoyed by all those aggressive swimmers. And do you remember Jonah? He tried his best to choke that whale slap to death.

And then there was Pinocchio. You remember Monstro, that perfectly delightful whale? Well, there he was, swimming around in the ocean, minding his own business, when Pinocchio's daddy sailed that boat right down his throat. Now, I'm gonna tell you the truth: when you swallow a whole sailboat, there ain't enough Rolaids on earth to help you.

Yes, sir. If you want to see folks get silly, just give 'em a cause to fight for. No more fishing? That's the silliest thing I ever heard of, and if we're going to keep this lunacy from sweeping the country, we've got to band together now.

The first person who walks up to you with an anti-fishing pamphlet, bust him right in the mouth and say something bad about his mama. Fishing and fishermen must be protected at all costs.

I don't know who started this craziness — sounds like the work of a worm.

Circle the Wagons, Boys

We hear stories all the time about how tough life was in the pioneer days, what with Indians, long cold winters and epidemics. But I'm here to tell you, fun-seekers, that I for one am not emotionally equipped to live in the eighties.

Now, I don't worry about the things that get most of us. I know there ain't nothing I can do about inflation, Afghanistan or ingrown toenails, so I don't worry too much about them, but the little aggravations are enough to make a person crave a persimmon.

It starts every morning when you get in your car and don't buckle your seat belt. It sounds like somebody guttin' a cat, what with the buzzers and lights going off.

I have to tell you, there is a special place in my heart for the old boy who thought of that buzzer, and I firmly believe that everything they say about his mama is true. And how about those safety inspection stickers on your car? If you want to see a policeman come unglued, just let him find one of those stickers with the hole punched in the wrong place.

And another thing. When I was a boy, if you wanted to kill a rat you got you a trap and a piece of cheese, you put it in the back of the cupboard, and by and by you killed yourself a rat. Boy, has all that changed! Now the government gives scientists a bunch of money and they spend it all trying to give that old mouse some kind of disease. Looks to me like the only thing having a rougher time in the eighties than people is the rats. I heard a story about a laboratory rat in Toronto last year. Seems they gave him more diet cola in a week than Orson Welles drinks in a year. On about the sixth day, the rat rolled over on his back, put his darling, little feet in the air, belched three times and shuffled off this mortal coil.

The list of 1980s aggravations just goes on and on — sales tax, income tax, computers, the surgeon general's report, car tags, dog tags, diets, exact change only.

It's enough to make you long for a good, old-fashioned Indian attack, isn't it?

Preacher Jackson Brings Home the Bacon

It seems that about all the news you read in the paper these days is bad. I sometimes just hate to pick up the paper because the news stories all depress me and the editorial page makes me mad; and the sooner Mary Worth starts to mind her own business, the better off we'll all be.

Little Abner and Pogo are both gone, and after twenty years Brenda Starr can't seem to settle down with that one-eyed fellow she married sometime back. Have you noticed that Brenda's husband seems to drown a lot?

All in all, the newspapers ain't what they used to be; but every once in a while, there's a story that makes it all worthwhile.

I read one the other day that made me feel good all over.

It seems that there's a preacher out in Pueblo, Colorado, by the name of Oliver Jackson. Now, everybody knows that preachers don't make much money, especially in a town like Pueblo, Colorado, which ain't big enough to have any major-league-type sinning going on.

So in order to save a little money, preacher Jackson got himself a yard full of pigs, sixty-seven in all. Everything was going good 'til the neighbors complained, and the city's animal shelter workers came out and seized all of the Rev's pigs.

Well, there was a great court battle that went on for three weeks. Now, all this time the city's animal shelter was giving them hogs room and board to the tune of $7,400. Well, bless Pat, the city lost the case and the judge ordered the city to pay the tab for keeping and feeding the pigs.

I'm sure the court's decision sounded real legal, but what it boils down to is, never fool with a potential ham hock, 'less you're willing to slop it.

To a Lady Who's Gone

With your permission, I would like to reminisce about a thing that I love very much. I'd like to remember a lady I grew up with who has passed away. I speak of a lady who is gone and can never return. I'm talking about the Atlanta that I grew up with. Now I know what you're saying. You're saying that the new Atlanta is the best Atlanta yet, and I can't disagree with that because I still love her above all cities. But somehow, when you get past forty, you long for things that can be no more. I love the new lady that is called Atlanta. It's a very special place to me, but somehow I can't help feeling a little sad at the death of the old Atlanta.

I remember when a family could ride the trolley to Rich's, get off and walk to the Paramount Theatre, and it would never occur to them that there was anything to be afraid of.

I remember when the best thing that could happen to a Sunday School class was for the teacher to take them to the old Rollerdrome for a night of roller skating.

I remember when a meal at the Pig and Whistle was the last word in a youngster's catalog of gourmet delights.

I remember when we thought the Hurt Building was a skyscraper. And when young boys gave adults their seats on a bus.

I remember when we went to Candler Field, not to catch an airplane, but hoping you would get to see an airplane take off.

I remember when the Southeastern Fair was the event of the year.

I remember when we could get a cherry Coke at any drugstore in town.

I remember when Bob Montag was the sports hero of every child in Atlanta.

I remember when the Atlanta Crackers would host a three-game series with the Birmingham Barons and sell out old Ponce de Leon Park all three nights.

Yes, sir, the old town's a lot bigger now; but you'd have a hard time convincing me that it's any better.

— from —

THE CORNBREAD CHRONICLES (1983)

ENGLISH IS A FOREIGN LANGUAGE

Changing Meanings

Have you ever noticed how our language is changing? So many new words and new meanings have crept into the language that, if we're not careful, we'll wake up one morning and won't be able to understand each other. Let me give you a few examples.

When did the color brown start to be known as earth tones, and why don't people say brown anymore?

When did a settee become a sofa, and whatever happened to davenports and chifforobes?

When did personality become charisma, and when did a he-man turn into a macho man?

When did dope fiends turn into junkies, and then into drug abusers? When did folks who drink too much turn into alcohol abusers? They are certainly not abusing alcohol; they are abusing their bodies. But nobody ever calls them body abusers.

When did dirty pictures become porn, and not-quite-so-dirty pictures become soft porn?

When did baseball teams become ominous? In my day, King Kong was ominous.

When did countries start being underdeveloped? Just a few years ago, Charles Atlas could take care of anything underdeveloped. And why are some countries called emerging nations, and how long before they quit emerging and become just regular ol' nations?

When did a used car become a pre-owned automobile, and when did a deodorant become an anti-perspirant?

When did fat girls become full-figured, and when did friendship become an interpersonal relationship?

When did a den become a great room, and when did a xylophone become vibes? And when did a split end become a wide receiver?

When did too much of anything become a glut? And when did the War Department become the Defense Department?

Yes sir, if this keeps up, someday you're going to need an interpreter to talk to your milkman.

Stupid Questions

Is it just my imagination, or are people asking more stupid questions than ever before?

For example, I pulled into a gas station the other day, and this ol' slack-jawed boy came walking out and said, "Can I do something for ya?" Now, bear in mind, I had just driven my car into his gas station, taken great care to get my tank close to his gas pump, and he says, "Can I do something for ya?" I said, "Yeah, I got this wisdom tooth that's been bothering me; can you take a look at it?" Now, that's not an extreme example, 'cause these things happen to me all the time.

I was fishing one day from a boat dock, and had caught a string of ten or twelve bream. While I was sitting there, a total stranger walked up, looked at my string of fish, and said, "Did you catch those fish?" I said, "No, actually I talked them into surrendering."

There was also the time my car overheated on the expressway about forty miles from any exit. The car was sitting there with steam coming out of everything; it looked like I was sitting in the middle of a giant London fog.

I was afraid the car was gonna blow up, so I got out of it and was standing there watching these clouds of steam boil out when a policeman pulled up. He said, "Are you having car trouble?" I said, "No, actually I was just about to steam some clams. Would you like to join me?"

You know what? I don't think that's any reason to put a man in jail.

Pebbles and Pops

It seems to me that television has changed the way we talk. Lately I've heard some things said that, years ago, you never would have heard anybody in the South say. Let me give you a few examples:

I heard a child the other day say he had a bag of shiny pebbles. Now, as a child, I knew what a pebble was. It was what people up north called small rocks. I never heard them referred to in the South as pebbles. I guess if I had been asked on a school test what a pebble was, I probably would have answered that it was a little bitty yankee rock.

Same thing applies to soft drinks. I was grown before I knew that a pop or a soda was nothing on earth but a Coca-Cola or a Pepsi or a Big Orange. I still don't know why they call 'em pop.

I asked a friend of mine from Pennsylvania, and he said they got that nickname for soft drinks because of the sound they make when you open them. That's the silliest thing I've ever heard of.

Anybody with the brain of a tire iron knows that soft drinks don't go "pop" when you open them; they go "whoosh." Champagne goes "pop." Weasels go "pop." But soft drinks go "whoosh."

Well, I guess things like that work themselves out, 'cause it would sound kind of strange to hear a teen-aged boy invite his girl out for a cold "whoosh."

Gimme a What?

I thought I had heard about everything there was, but I guess we live and learn. Seems that somebody in pro football decided the games would be more exciting if they wrote some new cheers for the cheerleaders. They said that "rah-rah" and "gimme an A" was O.K. for high school and college, but they thought pro cheerleaders were too sophisticated for that.

So the NFL has come up with an entirely new list of pro cheers. I thought you might enjoy hearing a few of them.

What do you think about this one? "Don't leave now, their defense we will wreck it. And if you stay till the third quarter, we'll all get naked." Or the one the Forty-Niners will be using soon: "Our team's great, our team's fine. Hey there, big boy, what's your sign?" Or this one from the Dallas cheerleaders: "Our clothes are tight, our modesty is less, but we sure love a man with an American Express."

I think one of my favorites is the Green Bay Packers' new one that goes, "Our Packers are rough, our Packers are tough, but it's kind of disgusting, 'cause they all dip snuff." Or this one, from a team I'd rather not identify: "Our team's just great, it has flavor. But keep an eye on the coach, 'cause he's a white slaver."

No wonder baseball is still the national pastime.

Chortling

Perfectly good words seem to be falling out of our language. I mean, one week a word is used, and the next week it's gone.

I tell you this with a heavy heart, because one of my favorite words has disappeared. It was always one of my favorites, but anytime I used it, people looked at me like I was some kind of a nut. The word is chortle. Think about that — a perfectly darling little word. I can't speak for anyone else, but I, for one, am very much into chortle.

When President Carter said, "I will never lie to you," a lot of folks sneered. Not me; I chortled. I chortled so much it made me sweat.

When the FBI caught those gravy-sucking congressmen in Abscam, I dang near made myself sick, chortling. When Richard Nixon said, "I'm not a crook," I fell out of my chair, chortling.

I come from a long line of chortlers. My uncle Enrico Porch was one of the world's first singing chortlers. As a matter of fact, he literally died chortling. You see, his wife asked him one day if he had it to do all over again, would he still marry her. He chortled, and she killed him with a nine iron. Which goes to prove what I've always said: Chortling at the wrong time will get you killed.

Language Barrier

It's a wonder to me that folks new to this country ever learned to speak the language. I mean, it's tough enough on those of us who have been here a long time, so think what a foreigner must have to go through trying to speak American.

For example, have you ever swoggled a horn? Now, think about that for a minute. When you say you have been hornswoggled, just what does that mean?

And what in the name of Lash LaRue is a galoot? And why do we consider people to be shiftless? Or have you ever in your entire life known anyone who buckled a swash? And why do we call longjohns, longjohns? Why not longfreds, or shortralphs? And why do we call a floozy a floozy?

Did you ever hear of a bushwhacker who whacked a bush? Or a guy who took the time to dry out a gulch? And while we're on the subject, what is a gulch? What is a pass, and why do they always cut people off there?

Why doesn't a cowboy say he'll cut them off at Whiteway and Main streets, or he'll cut them off just the other side of the Dairy Queen?

What do people mean when they say dagnabbit? And have you ever wondered why some people just leave, while others just mosey along? And some folks split, or cut out, or vamoose.

Yes siree, strangers in this country have a tougher time every year with the language. They must, 'cause I do.

Strange Things

Have you ever noticed all the strange things that happen in the world every day? If you stop and think about it, there's a lot of things going on that I don't think anybody understands.

For example, why is it that you never run out of Tabasco sauce? I can only assume, from that simple fact, that a small bottle of Tabasco sauce will last the average family a lifetime. That's strange.

Why is it that when you go into a gas station, you find that they have locked the bathroom and left the cash register unlocked? That strikes me as strange.

Why do musicians always say, "Take it from the top?" Seems to me, if they took it from the bottom, it would be a very short song.

Why do we call a hot water heater a hot water heater? Actually, it's a cold water heater. Doesn't that strike you as strange?

Why do professional air traffic controllers call themselves that? Does that mean that someplace there are amateur air traffic controllers?

Why do they sell life insurance at airports and not at bus stations? I find that strange.

Yes sir, the longer I live, the more I'm convinced that it's a strange, strange world.

A Brand-New Word

Have you heard the latest word to creep into our language? Are you ready for this? It's *bi-coastal*, and it refers to someone who spends a lot of time on each coast of the United States.

They invented it so that at a cocktail party you can say, "Oh, that's my friend Hazel. She's bi-coastal, you know." Now, I ask you, isn't that the most pretentious thing you've ever heard?

Well, I've decided our language can be greatly improved, if we come up with some more words that are just as pretentious as *bi-coastal*.

Here's my list, and maybe you can add to it:

Bi-drunk, as in "My friend Leon was bi-drunk last night." That means that Leon got drunk in two different beer joints.

Or how 'bout *bi-ugly*, as in "Eunice Mae is bi-ugly." That means Eunice Mae is twice as ugly as a two-day-old cantaloupe rind.

Or perhaps *bi-short*. That means that someone is so short, they have to stand in a chair to tie their shoelaces.

Or how 'bout *bi-crooked*. That means somebody is twice as crooked as John Dillinger, and in all likelihood is seeking public office.

What's Your Phobia?

I have been doing a little research about phobias, and I have discovered a very interesting fact. Did you know that almost everybody has some kind of phobia?

I started my research after reading a story about a lady in Tennessee who sued Knox County and the city of Knoxville for twenty-five thousand dollars. It seems that a wall-mounted toilet in the city-county building fell to the floor with her on it. The woman claimed, in her suit, that she now suffers from a fear of toilets, and is forced to search for toilets that are securely attached to the floor.

After reading this story, it occurred to me that a lot of folks have phobias that don't have names, and everyone knows that it's no fun having a nameless phobia. So I have set about to name some unnamed phobias.

For example, the lady I just told you about has *toilet phobia*. My Uncle Fergie has for years been afraid of his wife beating him up while he was asleep; he suffers from what I call *nocturnal knuckle phobia*. Here are a few more phobias that you need to know about:

Gazoonga phobia: an unnatural fear of bumping into Dolly Parton
Cosell phobia: a fear of long words with no meaning
Phobia aphobia: an unnatural fear of phobias
Formica phobia: a fear of sitting nude on a cold counter top
Claustrophobia: an unnatural fear of claustros

Dab phobia: a fear of Brillcream
Falsetto phobia: a fear of Slim Whitman

You may rest easy, my friends, for my research goes on. As a matter of fact, I am trying to name a phobia now that causes me to break into a cold sweat every time I hear the word Cleveland.

The Name Game

Who said, "What's in a name?" Whoever it was, I've forgotten his name. I do remember, however, that it's very important to pick the right name for your child. If you choose the wrong name, the child is going to be limited for the rest of his, or her, life. No matter how much talent, ambition or drive the child may have, it could be doomed to certain failure because of a badly chosen name.

Let me give you a few examples:

If, by chance, you named your son Rula, he could never be a professional wrestler, a lumberjack or a bartender.

If you named your son Fred, he could never grow up to own his own Chinese restaurant. I mean, how would a sign look that said, "Fred's Chinese Restaurant?"

If you named your daughter Hester, she could never grow up to be the belle of society. I know that 'cause the Vanderbilts had a bunch of children, and not a one of 'em was named Hester.

If you named your son Bruce, he could never grow up to be a hairstylist. I mean, after all, a guy named Bruce has got enough trouble. Right?

If you named your daughter Roxy, she could never grow up to be a ballerina.

So remember: You have an obligation to pick your child's name carefully. I should know, 'cause I'm Ludlow Porch.

Taking Orders

We get ordered around every day by absolute strangers, I mean, everywhere we go, we see signs that say Push, Pull, Exact Change Only, No Tank Tops, Authorized Personnel Only, Cash Only, No Smoking, Keep Off the Grass and on and on.

None of these orders bothers me much, but there's one that really does get my nanny goat. It affects every one of us, and it's high time we did something about it. It says, "Follow Label Instructions." Now, that just violates every concept of the American system.

How dare some stranger tell me that I must follow his directions! A person whom I know nothing about. He may not be from a good family, or he could be some kind of a wild, mad scientist, out to destroy nasal drip as we know it. Following this fella's instructions could be disastrous.

The instructions should say something like this: "Dear Customer, you bought this product. You paid for it with your hard-earned money. It is yours; you own it. Therefore, feel free to use it in any way that you like. Put it on your hair, if you want, or you might try rubbing it on your feet. Gargle with it, or put it on your fern. It's your property, dear customer, and we couldn't care less what you do with it."

When the free enterprise system comes out with a product with that kind of label, I'll be the first to buy it, and I won't care one way or the other whether it works or not.

Metric Nonsense

I haven't figured out the metric system yet, but I am sure about it — I'm sure I don't understand it, and I'm pretty sure nobody else does. It's the biggest mess since my cousin Doodle poured Karo syrup over his ant farm. The worst thing about the metric system is that it will kill some of our best clichés.

For example, do you remember how your grand-mother always said, "Give him an inch, and he'll take a mile?" You wouldn't have paid her a bit of attention, if she'd said, "Give him 2.5 centimeters and he'll take 1.69 kilometers." That just sounds silly.

And how about that ugly girl in your third-period history class? Nobody would say, "I wouldn't touch her with a three-meter pole."

Telling your girlfriend you love her a bushel and a peck is fine, but to say, "I love you a kilogram and a gram and a hug around the neck," would make you sound like a dang fool.

I'll tell you what I want to see. I want to see the first guy walk into Mr. Juhan's store and tell ol' Buford that he wants a liter of buttermilk, 'cause Buford is apt to cut him.

Wise Old Sayings

A lot of wise old sayings won't hold water when you examine them closely.

For example, I'm just tickled to death that life's not a bowl of cherries. Think about the implications of life being a bowl of cherries — it'll absolutely boggle your mind.

And how about this one — You always hurt the one you love. That's dumb, 'cause sometimes you hurt folks you don't give a damn about.

One of my least favorites is, Behind every dark cloud, there's a silver lining. That's just not so; behind a lot of dark clouds there is a tremendous rainstorm.

And anybody with a lick o' sense knows that a stitch in time will not save nine. A stitch in time will save six, tops.

Not only that, but an apple a day will dang near kill you.

And, too many cooks won't spoil the broth, 'cause broth ain't fit to eat in the first place.

Yes, sir, if you look at wise old sayings, you will find that a lot of them are just plain dumb.

Trivial Trivia

LUDLOW'S TRIVIA QUIZ

1. What was Burt Reynolds' name on *Gunsmoke*?
2. Who was the co-pilot in *The High and Mighty*?
3. What was the last line of *True Grit*?
4. In what movie did Bogart say, "Play it again, Sam?"
5. Who wrote "Gunga Din?"
6. Who were the announcers on "Burns and Allen?"
7. Who was Steve Allen's announcer on *The Tonight Show*?
8. What was Dr. Joyce Brothers' category on *The $64,000 Question*?
9. Name Buddy Hackett's television series.
10. Who was Horace McNalley?
11. Who wrote *Treadmill to Oblivion*?
12. Who played the original Trader Horn?
13. Name the Ida Lupino–Howard Duff series.
14. Who was Rod Redwing?
15. Who was heavyweight champion before Joe Louis?
16. On TV, who was "brave, courageous, and true?"
17. Who said, "We'll go on forever, 'cause we're the people"?
18. Who was the fictional hero of *The Maltese Falcon*?
19. What is Sugar Ray Robinson's real name?
20. Who was Jack Parr's band leader?
21. Name Long John Silver's parrot.
22. What kind of bird delivered Groucho's secret word?
23. Who was the radio sponsor of "Your Hit Parade"?

24. Name Kay Kyser's radio show.
25. Who sponsored the Ames Brothers' TV show?
26. Who coached Davis and Blanchard at West Point?
27. Who coached Jim Thorpe at Carlisle?
28. What was Mike Barnett against?
29. Who starred in *Dear Phoebe*?
30. Who was the monkey on *The Today Show*?
31. Name the nightclub in *Casablanca*.
32. Allen Hale, Jr., has had two series. Name them.
33. Who was host of "Welcome, Traveler?"
34. Name the ranch in *Red River*.
35. Who was the star of *Our American Cousin* the night Lincoln was shot?
36. Name Donald Duck's nephews.
37. Name Mickey Mouse's nephews.
38. Where did Steve Wilson work?
39. What was Mr. Belvedere's first name?
40. What was John Wayne's name in *Sands of Iwo Jima*?
41. Who played the title role in *The Stratton Story*?
42. What was the question that Jack Bailey asked every day on *Queen for a Day*?
43. Who was the "Queen of the Golden West"?
44. What was the name of Sky King's airplane?
45. Who played the Durango Kid?
46. Who was George Gobel's TV wife?
47. Who was his girl singer?
48. What was the name of Arthur Murray's TV show?
49. Who led three lives?
50. What singing group was featured on Bob Crosby's TV show?

51. Who said, "Nothing is so exhilarating as to be shot at without result?"
52. What was Peter Lorre's name in *The Maltese Falcon*?
53. What movie introduced Ma and Pa Kettle?
54. Who was Margaret Dumont?
55. Who was Andy Hardy's girlfriend?
56. Who played Henry Aldrich in the movies?
57. What is the full name of the Phantom's girlfriend?
58. Who played the albino in *God's Little Acre*?
59. What is Evel Knievel's first name?
60. What was the name of the taxi company on *Amos 'n' Andy*?
61. Who played Mr. Miniver?
62. Who was Teddy Nadler?
63. What was Jesse James' wife's name?
64. What was Hot-Shot Charlie's full name?
65. Where was the Heartbreak Hotel?

ANSWERS TO LUDLOW'S TRIVIA QUIZ

1. Quint Asper
2. John Wayne
3. "Come see a fat, old man, sometimes."
4. He never said it.
5. Rudyard Kipling
6. Harry Von Zell
7. Gene Rayburn
8. Boxing
9. *Stanley*
10. Stephen McNally's real name is Horace.
11. Fred Allen
12. Harry Caray, Sr.
13. *Mr. Adams and Eve*
14. He taught most Hollywood cowboys the fast draw.
15. Jim Braddock
16. Wyatt Earp
17. Ma Joad
18. Sam Spade
19. Walker Smith
20. Jose Melis
21. Captain Flint
22. A duck
23. Lucky Strike Cigarettes
24. "Kay Kyser Kollege of Musical Knowledge"
25. R.C. Cola
26. Red Blake
27. Pop Warner
28. Crime ("Man Against Crime")

29. Peter Lawford
30. J. Fred Muggs
31. Rick's Café American
32. *Casey Jones* and *Gilligan's Island*
33. Tommy Bartlett
34. The Red River D
35. Laura Keane
36. Huey, Dewey, and Louie
37. Morty and Ferdie
38. *The Illustrated Press*
39. Lynn
40. John Stryker
41. Jimmy Stewart
42. "Would you like to be queen for a day?"
43. Dale Evans
44. The Songbird
45. Charles Starret
46. Alice, played by Jeff Dunnell
47. Pretty, perky Peggy King
48. *Arthur Murray's Dance Party*
49. Herbert Philbrick
50. The Modernaires
51. Winston Churchill
52. Joel Cairo
53. *The Egg and I*
54. The foil of the Marx Brothers
55. Polly Benedict
56. Jimmy Lydon
57. Diana Palmer
58. Michael Landon

59. Robert
60. Fresh Air Taxi Company
61. Greer Garson
62. Big winner on several quiz shows in the fifties
63. Zee
64. Charles C. Charles
65. Down at the end of Lonely Street

THERE'S NOTHING NEAT ABOUT SEEING YOUR FEET (1984)

WAS MY FATHER REALLY A WATER BUFFALO?

There is probably no one reason that explains why some of us tend to double our weight every two meals while our more fortunate brothers and sisters can eat with both hands and still wear designer jeans. Over the years, I have tried every way possible to rationalize my fatness — perhaps to ease the mental pain of knowing that I have the willpower of a wino.

I once told my doctor that I thought I was over-weight because of my glands. He said there was no case in recorded, medical history where a man had two-hundred-pound glands. I hate snotty doctors.

Then I suggested to this same physician that my problem was hereditary. "I feel that's highly unlikely," he said, "unless you happen to be the off-spring of two love-crazed water buffaloes."

Not being one who discourages easily, I said "Well, Doc, maybe I just don't get enough exercise." He said that if I didn't cut back on my eating, a daily jog to Scandinavia wouldn't help. Like I said, I hate snotty doctors.

There are many other rationalizations, and I've tried them all. Some people use food as a tranquilizer; something goes amiss in their lives and they take it out on a coconut cake. Others eat for something to do with their hands; how many times have you sat watching television and suddenly realized that you've just finished off a twenty-five-pound bag of potato chips? Some people eat because they're bored or happy or have too much energy; still others eat because they're excited or unhappy or don't have enough energy.

But whatever the rationalization, the result is always the same: overweight. And once we cut through all the excuses, the real reason for our condition is that we simply eat too much of the wrong foods. It grieves me to say it, dear hearts, but I'm afraid it's true.

The best explanation I ever heard came from my friend Dennis's doctor. Dennis, who is five-nine and weighs about two hundred and thirty pounds, asked his doctor why he was so fat. "The answer is very simple," said his snotty doctor. "You're eating enough for two men, but the Good Lord blessed you with only one rectum."

The ultimate truism for us tubbos is that fat is often like good luggage — you keep it forever. That doesn't mean we have to stay fat; it just means that we have to be forever aware of what we're stuffing into that disposal below our noses.

My own particular downfall is bread. I honestly believe that if I had been born three thousand years ago, I would have rejected the sun god as a silly superstition and instead would have become the leader of a cult that worshipped bread.

In addition to bread, I also love potatoes. But even that could be an understatement. The truth of the matter is that I place potatoes on a pedestal right up there beside motherhood, Waylon Jennings and the Magna Carta. Potatoes are the only vegetable I know of that can be eaten three meals a day, seven days a week.

I enjoy butter, too, mainly because it goes so well with bread and potatoes. It also is delicious on all types of vegetables, and if you're on a real eating binge, butter can be eaten like ice cream.

Yes, sir, the willpower of a wino.

I SCREAM, YOU SCREAM,
WE ALL SCREAM ...

It would be interesting to find out how many over-weight people in the United States don't like ice cream. My guess is that it would be zero minus four. I suspect all are like me: They love the taste and flavors of ice cream, but eating it is also like a trip down memory lane.

When I was a small boy, ice cream was the ultimate treat. I never dreamed about owning a pony or dancing with a tight-sweatered cheerleader. I dreamed about my next Hunky (that's an Eskimo Pie, for our Northern readers).

I remember vividly how the alarm would be sounded. It was the obligation and duty of the first child who spotted the Hunky Man to alert the neighborhood of his presence. This was done by screaming at the top of your lungs, "HUNKY MAN!" The cry would be picked up by your young friends, and immediately every child in earshot was looking or begging for a nickel.

The more prudent youngsters had advance stashes of nickels and therefore did not have to waste precious seconds explaining to their mamas that "one little Hunky won't hurt my supper."

Once you reached the Hunky Man, you found him surrounded by every child you ever knew. A crowd four or five deep would circle around the white pushcart that was filled with dry ice and various ice cream treats.

The kids who had been unable to come up with a

nickel always hung around hoping to talk their best friends into just one lick. One sure-fire method for discouraging these whiners was to spit on your ice cream.

It was the middle-class kids who were always eating the five-cent Hunkies. Rich children, on the other hand, could afford a dime Dreamsicle. I was thirty years old before I tried a Dreamsicle. On the rare occasions when I had a dime, I felt it made more sense to buy two Hunkies than one Dreamsicle.

The girls in the neighborhood always bought a cup of ice cream because it had a picture of a movie star inside on the cardboard lid. All they had to do was lick the ice cream off the lid and there was a picture of Shirley Temple, Lon McAlister or, if you got lucky, maybe even George Brent.

Hunkies, however, had their surprises, too. If you found a star under the ice cream on your Hunky stick, you won a free one.

Secretly I always suspected that the Hunky Man was heavily involved in organized crime. You see, I must have eaten well over ten thousand Hunkies in my day, and I never found a star or knew anybody who did. It grieves me to think it, but this scam obviously was the work of the Mafia.

Ice cream has always been an important part of my life. One of the best jobs I ever had was as a soda jerk. It was such a good job, in fact, that I had to serve an apprenticeship to get it.

The apprenticeship had nothing to do with jerking

sodas. The only time the apprentice went behind the counter was to shave ice. This was a tough job, accomplished by putting a fifty-pound block of ice in a washtub and cutting it into small pieces with a four-pronged ice shaver.

All other times, the main job of the apprentice was delivering prescriptions on a bicycle. I spent ninety percent of my time peddling and ten percent praying that the soda jerk would die so I could take his job.

When I was finally made a full-time soda jerk, one of the things that thrilled me most was the uniform. It consisted of a white apron that went from waist to shoes, and a snow-white, heavily starched jacket. This magnificent ensemble was topped off by a white, starched garrison cap and a black leather bow tie.

My fame as a soda jerk soon spread. Not only did I look as sharp as a King Hardware pocket knife, but I also took great pride in the wonders that I created behind that beautiful, marble counter.

I still remember the formula for my perfect fountain Cokes: a glass full to the brim with shaved ice, one and a half squirts of Coca-Cola syrup, topped off with carbonated water. The secret was in the syrup. The perfect fountain Coke had to have exactly one and a half squirts of syrup.

My real forte was the now-famous Ludlow Luscious Banana Split. This was made by carefully slicing a banana lengthwise and putting it on each side of an oblong glass dish. In the middle of the dish I placed three scoops of ice cream — one vanilla, one chocolate and one strawberry.

These were then generously covered with strawberries, pineapple and nuts. The entire masterpiece was finally topped off with whipped cream and a cherry.

Once properly prepared, the Ludlow Luscious Banana Split was a meal in itself. This gourmet delight cost twenty-five cents, but I can assure you it was worth every penny.

If you're wondering why you haven't been able to get a good banana split in recent years, allow me to offer my theory about the unfortunate demise of this American delicacy.

In the first place, soda jerks no longer wear the proper uniform. How can we possibly expect a decent banana split from someone not wearing a black leather bow tie? They also don't wear the starched, white garrison caps anymore. I think long hair forced that change. (I'm sure you remember that period when most teenaged boys looked like chrysanthemums.)

In the second place, banana splits are no longer served properly. Styrofoam containers and plastic spoons are outrageous. To get the full taste of every mouthful, it is absolutely mandatory that banana splits be eaten out of a glass container with a metal spoon.

It grieves me deeply to think that a full generation has come along without knowing the ecstasy involved in eating a banana split worthy of its name.

The history of ice cream is long and glorious. No one is exactly sure how long this fattening delicacy has been around, but there is evidence that three thousand years ago the Chinese were mixing snow with fruit juice.

In 1295, Marco Polo brought ice cream recipes back to Venice from Peking. And by 1700, ice cream had become a popular dessert among rich, American colonists.

Records show that during the summer of 1790, George Washington spent more than two hundred dollars with a New York ice cream merchant. That may not sound like a lot of money today, but it becomes a monstrous amount when you realize that in 1790 land could be bought for ten cents an acre. Twenty years later, Dolly Madison was serving ice cream at the White House.

On a bright summer day in 1846, a breakthrough occurred that would change the course of history for ice cream eaters. It was on that day that Nancy Johnson invented the hand-cranked freezer.

In my opinion, there should be monuments in honor of this great woman. There should be highways, parks and cities named for her. There should be a Nancy Johnson golf tournament, a Nancy Johnson First Baptist Church and at least one Willie Nelson album bearing her name.

Without her invention, countless meetings with dinner on the grounds would have been disappointing. Without her I wouldn't have known Uncle Chuck's homemade peach ice cream, and millions of kids wouldn't know the thrill of licking a dasher.

History may have forgotten her, but I never will. On behalf of all children and all fat folks of the world, I say to Nancy Johnson, inventor of the hand-turned ice cream freezer, "Thanks for the memories."

SHOPPING AT FULTON TENT AND AWNING

One of the first indications that you've joined the ranks of the overweight is that your clothes no longer fit. That means when you finally manage to get the buttons through the holes, you have trouble breathing and your face begins to turn blue.

So then you go out and buy new, larger clothes (the old ones probably shrunk in the dryer), but no matter how much you spend, they just don't seem to look very good. For years I blamed my sartorial problems on clothing manufacturers; they just don't make attractive clothes for overweight people, I said.

Finally I had to break down and admit that it wasn't the clothes, fun-seekers. I was just too fat to look good in anything.

Like most fat folks, I made jokes about my weight to soften the blow. "I buy all my clothes from Fulton Tent and Awning," was one of my favorites. Or, "I'll just slip into a shower curtain and be right over." But in fact, shopping for clothes when you're into the super large sizes is about as much fun as falling down a flight of stairs.

The first problem you encounter is that most regular clothing stores don't carry a very good selection of large sizes. In men's clothing, you're lucky to find anything bigger than a size forty-eight on the rack, and most of them are about as stylish as zoot suits.

Faced with the option of becoming a nudist, you

choose instead to go to a store for big men. The advantage of these stores is that they usually have a good selection of attractive clothes. The disadvantages, however, are enough to make a porpoise frown.

For openers, a shirt which cost fifteen dollars in a regular clothing store will cost you close to forty in a big men's store. There ain't that much more material in a size fifty-two than there is in an extra-large.

Then there are the clerks, who for some reason are always skinny. Having a skinny clerk in a fat man's store is like having a dentist work on your in-grown toenail. They just don't seem to grasp the problems of being overweight.

For example, they'll take your measurements and then announce in a voice loud enough for everyone in the store to hear, "Well, sir, it looks like you're going to need a size fifty-two portly." I, for one, would rather be called a fat bastard than to be called portly. I could settle for husky, obese, fat or even lard bucket, but never, ever portly.

If you shop in a store for big men or women, there are certain universal rules which should be followed when buying clothes. I call these "Ludlow's Rules for Hiding It and Keeping It Hidden," and I'm glad to share them with you:

1. *Never tuck your shirt or blouse into your trousers or skirt.*

There are no exceptions to this rule. If you're fat, your best bet is to try and camouflage it. Tucking your shirt into your pants only emphasizes that you don't have a waist. Go instead for the loose look.

I used to know a young lady who, during her high school days, had a cute figure and dressed to show off the assets Mother Nature had bestowed upon her. When she got out of high school and entered the workforce, however, she cut back on her exercise but not on her eating. The high school figure that she used to emphasize was gone almost overnight. Unfortunately, my friend didn't notice that the sand had shifted in her hour-glass figure, so she continued to dress the same way she always had.

I can only assume that she thought the metric system was in some way responsible for the difference in the sizes of her clothes, and that humidity had warped all the mirrors on the face of the earth.

She continued wearing tight clothes with wide belts, just as she had when she weighed fifty pounds less, and she tucked in all her blouses. The result was that she looked like she was wearing a money belt filled with Talmadge hams.

2. *Never wear a bathing suit.*

This shouldn't require any explanation. There's room enough in this world for only one great white whale, and Moby Dick is filling that spot.

3. *Never wear horizontal stripes.*

This is an old, tested rule for fat folks. Suffice it to say that wearing horizontal stripes makes us look like football fields.

4. *Never wear tank tops.*

At the very best, tank tops are tacky on a skinny person. On a heavy man or woman, they make the wearer look like a ten-pound sausage in a five-pound skin. They're a disaster.

5. *Never wear short pants.*

This rule applies to both men and women. A fat man in Bermuda shorts, invariably accompanied by black socks and wing-tip shoes, is one of the silliest sights in the world. I personally think such dress is responsible for the unfortunate decline of Miami Beach.

A fat lady in shorts is awful no matter what kind of socks or shoes she wears. She looks bad enough coming towards you; going away, you get the illusion of two cats in her shorts fighting for their very lives.

6. *Avoid wearing jeans.*

Jeans are made for those who are slim of hip and lean of belly. So if you're built more like Orson Welles than James Stewart, forget about jeans, designer or otherwise. There ain't nothing you can write on the back pockets that will make you look any better in a pair of jeans.

7. *Do not wear tennis dresses.*

Fat men in tennis dresses are a little more than suspect. Fat women in tennis dresses are ridiculous; they look like they're wearing an umbrella tied at the waist.

8. *Avoid large belt buckles.*

With the urban cowboy craze came what I call the belt buckle craze. Men all over America started wearing large, silver belt buckles, which said things like "Lone Star State" or "Sam's Truck Stop."

Most of these buckles are about four inches by three inches, and some fat men think they make them look slimmer. The truth is that they make 'em look like they're wearing the grill of a '51 Hudson around their waists.

9. *Don't wear high heels.*

Fat men wearing high heels don't look any taller, but they do send out a message to the world: "I'm fat, but I hope that by wearing high heels you won't notice that I'm also short."

Fat women in high heels likewise don't look any slimmer; they just look a lot more uncomfortable. I always wonder how long they can maintain their balance.

10. *Never wear bikini underwear.*

Wearing bikini underwear can be very dangerous for people who are overweight. If you were in an accident and taken to an emergency room for treatment, you could die while the doctors and nurses stood around the room laughing at how silly you look in bikini underwear.

HAS ANYBODY SEEN MY ELEPHANT?

A DIETER'S PRAYER

This is my prayer as I contemplate my belly: Dear Lord, please save me from doughnuts with jelly. And Lord, please keep me from that fattening brew — Budweiser, Pabst and Miller Lite, too.

Please, Lord, stop my craving for my wife's homemade bread, and help me to realize that it's all in my head. Take away my yearning for a big juicy steak and, above all, the things that the baker bakes.

Hear my prayer, O Lord, each word as it's given, so someday I'll look just like David Niven.

O Lord, hear this prayer, each word that I utter, and if you're really listening, Lord, please pass the butter.

When all else has failed — the exercise and all the gimmicks — there's only one thing left for a fat person to try. A diet.

As I said earlier, I have been on many diets in my lifetime. In fact, I have lost more than fifty pounds more times than I remember, and all told I have lost more than two thousand pounds. But take my word that my battle is not over yet.

Nonetheless, dear reader, I want to share with you some of the more successful diets that I have tried.

Dr. Brezil's Famous Fish Diet
This diet is based on eating a lot of protein. You eat

broiled fish three meals a day. I lost weight trying it, but after a week I had an uncontrollable craving for worms. I don't recommend this diet unless you own stock in a bait shop.

Diet Pills

I've had some good results with pills. For awhile they seem to kill my appetite and cut down on my craving for fattening foods. I also noticed that they give me a lot of energy. Once, for no good reason, I found myself painting my garage at four o'clock in the morning. Another time I caught myself driving seventy-five miles an hour down Peachtree Street, and I wasn't in any particular hurry.

Dr. Feldman's Diet

On this diet, you can have anything you want to eat. The only stipulation is that you must hold your breath the entire time you're eating. I lost a good deal of weight on Dr. Feldman's diet, but I never got used to fainting.

The Porch Elephant Diet

I invented this one myself, and it's a sure-fire way to lose weight. You can eat one elephant a week, cooked any way you like, but you must catch it yourself and kill it with a butter knife. I found that after the first week I just laid around on the living room floor with a butter knife in my hand, screaming for elephants. For variety after the first week, you may substitute a cocker spaniel for the elephant.

Weight Watchers

This is truly a fabulous diet. The first time I tried it, I was faithful and lost about sixty pounds in a relatively short period of time. The good thing about Weight Watchers is that you get enough to eat while you're dieting.

In addition to the diet, they try to teach behavior modification; that means they try to teach you to stop eating like you're going to the electric chair.

I must admit I was less successful with my behavior modification. My first day off the diet, I ate the First Methodist Church in Snellville and two tickets to a Conway Twitty concert.

The Ex-Lax Diet

This is another diet I invented. The advantage of it is that you can eat anything you want — bread, butter, potatoes, cakes, pies or whatever. The only drawback is that along with your meal you must eat a full box of Ex-Lax.

The secret to this diet is that although you can eat anything you want, after three days you're too weak to walk to the table. This diet comes with two guarantees: (1) You will lose weight, and (2) You will end up in the hospital. Check your hospitalization plan before trying this diet.

The Drinking Man's Diet

This diet calls for drinking a fifth of Jack Daniels thirty minutes before each meal. You may not lose much weight, but you'll experience many happy hours.

The truth is that alcohol is very caloric. For example, a beer with four percent alcohol has roughly two hundred calories per twelve ounces. Three cans of that will knock a hole clean through a 1,500-calorie-per-day diet.

The same is true of wine. At eighteen percent alcohol, you're looking at about 165 calories per one-half cup. If you're one of those who drinks straight from the bottle, you're in trouble.

Gin, rum, vodka and whiskey, which are about eighty-six proof, contain about seventy calories per shot. That may not sound like much, but don't forget the calories in the mixers.

My boyhood friend Snake Burnett was very weight conscious, but Snake couldn't do without a little snort everyday. So he searched far and wide for a diet that would allow him to drink. He asked his doctor about it, and the doctor suggested that he get lots of exercise. That posed another problem for old Snake, 'cause he hated exercise more than Nixon hated tape recorders.

The only regular exercise Snake ever got was fist fighting on Friday nights at Monk Gregory's Billiard Palace. So Snake wrote a letter to the trainer of the Ohio State wrestling team and asked him to estimate how many calories were burned up in an average fist fight.

With that information in hand, Snake quickly calculated that if he got into two fist-fights and one riot, he could drink one fifth of whiskey and one six-pack of beer per weekend without gaining weight.

Snake forgot to calculate how many more calories would be burned up as the police beat him senseless, but by then it really didn't matter anyway. One thing he did learn, however, is that a blackjack upside the head usually will kill an appetite.

The Yogurt Diet

This is one of the most disgusting diets I have ever run across. The name alone should tip you off. Just say it out loud — YOGURT. It sounds more like a bodily function than a food.

Besides that, if fat people liked yogurt they probably wouldn't be fat in the first place.

This diet was developed by Willetta Warburg, a food editor, and Rose Mirenda, a nutritionist. It gives you a seven-day menu that is high in lean protein and low in cholesterol, saturated fats and refined carbohydrates (that's Twinkies, for those of you who don't like science).

For example, here's one day's menu that contains about a thousand calories:

Breakfast — One small glass of prune juice; one container of plain yogurt; one slice of whole wheat toast; one small pat of margarine; one plain cup of coffee or tea.

Mid-morning Snack — Four dried apricot halves.

Dinner — Four canned sardines, drained of oil; one-half hard-cooked egg; a wedge of lettuce; a slice of tomato; one slice of whole wheat toast; one cup of plain coffee or tea.

Mid-afternoon Snack — A container of plain yogurt.

Supper — Three slices of breast of chicken, baked or broiled or stewed, plus the liver; one-half cup of cooked spinach; one-fourth cup of rice; one cup of plain coffee or tea.

Bedtime Snack — One glass of skim milk.

That, fun-seekers, is probably the most tasteless diet ever devised. After a full week of eating this, you would not only hate plain yogurt, but you'd also probably hate America, the works of George Gershwin and your mama.

The Blue Diet

On this diet, you can eat all the blue food you want. The catch is that there isn't any blue food.

Man, of course, has created enough dyes to make anything blue, but Mother Nature, in her infinite wisdom, did not see fit to make any food naturally blue. No, not even blueberries; they're actually purple, and there's no blue in the meat of the blue fish.

So go ahead — eat all the blue food you want.

CAN I JUST DO IT TIL I NEED GLASSES? (1985)

MAKING MONEY AND TIME AT GLOVER'S PHARMACY

I don't think my boyhood crowd was any more industrious than today's youngsters, but I do believe the times made us more aware of money. There was literally no money around to be shared with us by our parents, so if we were going to have any spending loot, it was up to us to make it.

One of my first ventures was selling figs, which grew abundantly on bushes in our yard. I would pick the figs and sell them door-to-door for ten cents a quart. If I worked hard, I could make about two dollars a week. That was big money to me, and I probably would have done it year 'round and grown rich. But, of course, the figs wouldn't cooperate.

I collected and sold soft drink bottles at two cents a piece, but that required a lot of bending over. I tried cutting grass for awhile, but that was highly competitive and also seasonal. I was looking for steady income.

One summer my Uncle Harry and two of his friends got an *Atlanta Constitution* paper route and needed somebody to help them. I fell heir to a new job.

The job was fun and paid pretty well. I particularly liked being with the big boys, and being out on the streets before daylight was an exciting and wonderful thing. And best of all, breakfast was also furnished.

Let me explain. It wasn't a real breakfast, like bacon and eggs; it was a special breakfast. We knew that on Mondays, for example, the Dutch Oven bakery left doughnuts at Mrs. Brown's house, so we helped ourselves. Also on Mondays, the milkman left chocolate milk at another door and orangeade at yet another. We simply walked around the neighborhood checking front porches. We would then sit under the street light at Spring and Maple Streets and breakfast like European royalty. Then we would throw our paper and bottles down the sewer and deliver our papers.

I'll never understand how we did that every morning and never got caught.

I assume the poor neighbors thought they were being shorted by the delivery man, when all the while four young hellions were eating like kings. We were growing fat and the delivery guys were catching hell.

I can only hope for two things: (1) that none of them got into too much trouble because of our actions, and (2) that the statute of limitations has run out on the four young breakfast thieves.

In my youth, I sold cloverine salve. One day I was look-ing in the back of a comic book and saw an ad for cloverine salve. It said that you could sell salve and not only make big money but win terrific prizes. You could win a single-shot .22 rifle, a bicycle and, if you sold enough, even a pony.

My God, I thought, my very own pony.

I cut the coupon out and mailed it that very day. In about two weeks, my first supply of salve came back. It was a long, cardboard tube and contained ten cans of cloverine salve. It also contained ten pictures of the Last Supper, suitable for framing. The accompanying letter said I could give away one picture with every can of salve that I sold. The letter also said that I was to sell the salve and send the money back, and then I could get more salve to sell.

I sold my first ten cans in about two days. I sent the money and sure enough, I got a new order in the mail.

I was less enthusiastic about the sales of the second batch. School had started and I was busy with my friends. Besides, I had already sold salve to all my relatives.

I didn't bother to respond to the company's first let-ter. It said they were disappointed in my sales results, and that if my present rate of sales continued, it was apparent that I was going to have to face the balance of my youth without the benefit of a pony.

The letter didn't bother me much, however, because it was already obvious to me that there was a glut of cloverine salve on the market. Every kid I knew was selling it. You couldn't go into any house in my neighborhood without seeing at least one picture of the Last Supper. Besides, my mama had already told me that if I won a pony, I'd have to keep him in my room. I didn't know a whole lot about ponies, but I knew they had disgusting personal habits that would make them impossible as roommates.

Their second letter was a little more emphatic. It indicated that I'd stolen their salve and my heart pumped peepee. They said that prison was too good for me, and that if they didn't get either their salve or their money back, they were going to come to East Point, Georgia, and take whatever steps were necessary to protect their interest.

I remember thinking, They're coming all the way from New York to collect their $2.50. They're probably going to send a hit man. He'll shoot me down like the dog I am. Where am I going to get $2.50? It's too late to send them back their salve. I'm doomed.

I worried and fretted for days but nothing happened. I never heard from them again, and I guess if I haven't heard from them since 1944, I'm safe now.

I was fortunate enough after that to get several of what I considered to be dream jobs.

My first dream job was at the swimming pool. Somehow, I was able to talk myself into a job as a locker boy. I carried the key to all the lockers, and when the swimmers came in from the pool, they would scream, "Locker Boy! Locker Boy!" and I would go open their lockers.

I had thought a job at the pool would be real glamorous. I would get a good tan and the girls would be falling at my feet. The only problem was that I never got to see any girls in the boys' locker room. And I never even got to see the water, let alone the sunshine. It left much to be desired as a glamorous job.

My next job was at Glover's Pharmacy, where I had applied for a job as a soda jerk. It was explained to me, however, that you did not start as a soda jerk. You started as a delivery boy and worked your way up to the position of soda jerk.

A delivery boy in those days needed his own bicycle and had to be able to make change. He also needed to be willing to peddle his butt off in all kinds of weather for thirty cents an hour, plus tips. I did it for almost a year and never got a tip.

Of course, the thing that kept me going was not the money. The carrot at the end of my stick was the job as soda jerk.

I used to fantasize aloud as I was peddling up a long hill in the rain: "Maybe when I get back, I'll find out there has been a robbery at the drug store and the soda jerk has gone down in a hail of bullets. When I get back, his bullet-riddled body will already be in the process of being embalmed at Hemperly's Funeral Home. I'll ride up on my bike and Doc Glover will say, 'OK, kid. You're our new soda jerk. Put on your uniform and start making your way in life.'"

In my fantasy, I would then go in the back room and put on my freshly starched, snow-white Ike jacket.

Then my clean, white apron and gleaming, white soda jerk cap. Then last, but not least, I would put on my black leather bow tie.

My fantasy continued with buxom cheerleader types coming in and ordering chocolate nut sundaes, slurping them down and then offering me their bodies in payment for their soda fountain bills.

That particular part of the fantasy helped me to hang in there until I finally got the job. The soda jerk didn't even die in a hold-up; his daddy made him quit when his grades plummeted.

I got my uniform and then sat back and waited for the girls to come in and throw themselves at my feet.

The first night I was there, it seemed as though my every prayer was being answered. In the front door of Glover's Pharmacy walked the most beautiful girl that had ever sucked down a fountain Coke. Not only was she beautiful and built like a brick chicken coop, she also was the head majorette at Russell High School.

What the heck if she was three years older than I was. I liked older women. Besides, only older girls knew how to appreciate a man in uniform.

As she wriggled up to the counter, I said, "Hi!"

"Hi!" she said. "Can you get me a chocolate shake?"

"My specialty," I said. Things couldn't be better, I thought. I'll make her a chocolate shake so thick she'll have to get a friend to help her chew it. Once she tastes my shake, she's mine forever. I'll quit this job and we'll run off to Daytona Beach.

Watching her drink that shake was wonderful. As a

matter of fact, just watching her breathe caused most of my Presbyterian training to go right down the toilet.

She finished her shake after what seemed to be an eternity.

"Was the shake OK?" I asked.

She said it was wonderful. Then she added, "Can I say something personal to you?"

I thought, Here it comes; she's making her move. Trying to remain calm and act like Clark Gable, I said, "Sure, you can tell me anything."

She batted her eyes and said in a whisper, "If you use Noxzema every day, it'll really help your pimples. I know, 'cause my face used to look a lot worse than yours." Then she said bye-bye, swung on her penny loafers, and strolled out of my life forever.

That episode took a great deal of the romance out of my soda jerk job. I felt like my future as a lover was over. I had been to the mountaintop and the mountaintop was closed.

I had a couple of other good jobs after that. I was a lifeguard for a summer. I got a great tan and got to row a boat around the pool and blow my whistle at little kids who were running, but the harem I had hoped for was always gone when the pool closed at ten o'clock at night.

I also sold ice cream from a pushcart. That job lasted almost a full day. The cart was heavy and the money was short, and the only chance for advancement was to move up to a bigger, heavier pushcart. I passed.

Later, I worked as an usher at every movie theater in

the Tri-City area. I liked that job a lot; I got to see free movies and meet a lot of girls, even if I never could sit with them. It also helped me to become a pretty fair country trivia player, which has since paid far more handsomely than the job ever did.

HAPPINESS IS A BEST-SELLING TITLE

My boyhood friend, Lardo Dupree, got interested in music when we were in high school. He saved the money he made from his paper route and bought a guitar.

Lardo was soon playing in talent shows and was starting to build a local reputation. His big chance finally came when he was seventeen. He was invited to New York to try out for the Ted Mack show.

His mother worked around the clock to make him a costume, and it was a sight to behold. It was a black cowboy suit with about fifty thousand sequins sewn all over it, and across the back in big, sequined letters with little musical notes all around it was "LARDO." It was a sight.

Lardo's daddy took a magic marker and wrote "Lardo Dupree" on his guitar in a fancy script. To top off the entire outfit, they bought Lardo a white cowboy hat and a pair of bright red, high-heeled cowboy boots.

He was a sight — all 5'3", 260 pounds of him.

You could tell at a glance that not only was he ready to conquer *The Ted Mack Original Amateur Hour,* he was ready to take New York by storm.

Unfortunately, network television never got to see Lardo or his outfit.

On the way to the TV station, Lardo was set upon by a group of ruffians who dragged him into a New York alley and beat him senseless. His guitar was broken, his white cowboy hat and red boots were stolen, and his cowboy suit was thrown into the Hudson River. Unfortunately, Lardo was wearing the cowboy suit at the time.

Lardo came home heavy-hearted and tried to pick up the pieces of his broken career. He even wrote a song about his experience. It was called "I Wish to Hell They'd Bomb Ol' Broadway." The song never caught on.

Lardo's experience in that New York alley had a profound effect on him. He still wanted to be in show business, but his taste for singin' and pickin' had been all but eliminated.

He decided that if he indeed had any future in show business, it would have to be as a songwriter. That way he could write his songs and let somebody else go to New York wearing sequins and be beaten up and thrown into the Hudson River.

To keep body and soul together, he took jobs in small country and western clubs. But Lardo soon realized that he didn't like the night life. So he took a job with a band that was traveling all over the Southeast playing country fairs. But the band broke up and Lardo got stranded in Tupelo, Mississippi, and had to wire his daddy for money to get home.

He came home and made his parents a promise that he would settle down. They made him swear that he would get a "real job" and give up show business forever.

They wanted him to join the First Baptist Church, become a Mason like his daddy, and then find a good Christian girl to settle down with. Lardo wanted to tell them what they wanted to hear, and he wanted to do all the things that would make them happy.

Underneath all his promises, however, he wondered if he could ever give up show business as long as he was a failure.

On the other hand, he was tired of the many disappointments he had experienced. Maybe they were right. Maybe he would be happier if he gave it all up.

He decided to give their way a shot. What the hell — what had he ever gotten out of show business? Just a lot of heartache and a wet cowboy suit.

He made a promise to his parents that he was home to stay and that they could quit worrying about him, 'cause from that day forward he was going to become a pillar of the community.

The next Sunday when Brother Warr gave the altar call at the church, old Lardo hit the center aisle. Everybody in the church was squallin'. They had decided years ago that Lardo was going to be a worthless, no-account guitar picker for the rest of his life and, Praise the Lord, there he was, shakin' hands and huggin' the preacher and accepting Jesus Christ as his personal Lord and Savior.

The very next Sunday he was baptized. The preacher put him under four times — one extra to get all that show-business sin off him. Lardo was cleansed down to the bottom of his guitar-pickin' heart.

The next step on the ladder of respectability was a job. Lardo's daddy said, "What you gonna do about a job, son?"

"I'm just gonna watch the want ads and see what turns up," he said.

"Lardo, you got any clothes that you can wear on a job interview?"

"What's wrong with the clothes I'm wearing, Daddy?"

"Son, folks just don't go on a job interview wearing clothes that got sequins all over them, and besides, them britches ain't never fit right since you got baptized in 'em. I think they shrunk about three sizes. Can you breathe all right in them pants, son?"

Lardo said, "Daddy, I've been in show business so long that I ain't got no civilian clothes. Just about everything I own has some kind of sequin flowers or musical notes on them."

Lardo's daddy said, "Well, I can't have you out here looking for a job in them funny clothes. We'll just make us a little trip down to Robert Hall and pick you up some decent clothes."

When they left the Robert Hall store, old Lardo looked just like a chubby Adolph Menjou.

It took Lardo about a week, but he finally found a

job. He answered an ad in the paper, and after three weeks of training, Lardo became our town's first Fuller Brush man.

His mama and daddy couldn't have been any prouder if he had been elected pope.

It soon became evident to all of the single girls in town that not only was Lardo Dupree back to stay, but he was also one of the town's most eligible bachelors. I mean, what else could a girl want in a man?

There was old Lardo not only freshly baptized in the church, but rumor had it that he was in line to become deacon. When you combined that with the fact that he was a full-fledged Fuller Brush man and owned two Robert Hall suits (one blue and one brown), he was what the girls' mothers liked to refer to as "a catch."

Every Wednesday night you could hear all the mothers talking after prayer meeting.

"Why, did you hear that prayer that Lardo prayed tonight?"

"I do believe that was the sweetest thing I ever heard."

"And did you see that suit he was wearin'? I bet it cost fifty dollars if it cost a dime."

"Don't you know his mama is proud of him. Why, Lawde, any woman in town would be proud to have him as a son-in-law, him being a Fuller Brush man and all."

"Do you know what I heard? I heard that on his sample case he's got his initials right on the side."

"You don't mean it?"

"That's what I heard. Right on the side. A big L.D.

plain as anything."

"Say what you want to, he's by far the best dresser in church."

"Word is he buys all his shirts at Gallant Belk. Not only that, but he sends all his shirts out to be washed."

It was inevitable. Lardo didn't stand a chance. Within six months he was engaged, and three months later he again hit the center aisle of the First Baptist Church. This time with Helen Winston on his arm. The whole ceremony took nine minutes and fifteen seconds. Lardo had married the daughter of the county school superintendent and, what was more important to his parents, had taken one more step on the road to total respectability.

To most people, Lardo appeared to be a happy man. Even his mama and daddy thought that their baby had at last settled down. Lardo and Helen had been married now for almost two years, and to the world it appeared that the conversion of Lardo Dupree was complete.

Then one night Helen missed Lardo. She looked all over the house. She finally found him sitting on a stump behind the smokehouse with his guitar trying to remember all the words to the immortal "There Stands the Glass," as sung by Webb Pierce.

Helen didn't think anything about it. She just said, "Lardo, what you doin' out here in the dark with that old guitar? Don't you know you're missin' *Peyton Place* on TV?"

Lardo didn't try to explain, he just said, "Comin', Helen."

Helen didn't even think anything was amiss when she found a copy of Roy Clark's Big Note Guitar Lessons that Lardo had ordered through the mail.

The next day Lardo came home wearing a pair of red cowboy boots.

Helen said, "Why, Sugar, it looks funny for a Fuller Brush man to be wearing red cowboy boots."

Lardo explained it away by saying, "Helen, it's the latest fashion. You ain't nobody unless you're wearin' cowboy boots. That Hollywood fellow started it all. You know who I'm talking about, the one in *Urban Cowboy*, that John Ravolta, or whatever his name is."

Nobody in town had any idea that Lardo was the most miserable man who ever sold Fuller Brushes while wearing red cowboy boots.

He was sick of selling door-to-door. He was sick of Robert Hall and his damn suits. He was sick of his life in general. Deep down in his guts, he knew that he was born to be in show business, and it was an easy matter for him to despise anything or anybody that he thought was conspiring to change what he knew was his destiny.

Helen had set the clock radio to go off at 8:30. She reasoned that they were due at Sunday school at 10:00 and that would give them an hour and a half.

She was not surprised that Lardo was not sleeping beside her. Sometimes on Sunday morning he would get the paper and read it while he was drinking a cup of coffee.

She went right to her shower and did not notice the note on the sink until she was drying her hair. It was in an envelope that had her name on the outside.

The note said:

You people are driving me crazy. I'm going to Nashville. I'll send for you, but I don't much care whether you come or not.

Signed,

Lardo

P.S. Your mama ought to be in a cage.

When the folks in town found out that Lardo was missing, the reaction was wide and varied.

Preacher Warr said, "May God be with him."

His daddy-in-law said, "God wouldn't be caught in the same county with that white trash."

Lardo's mother-in-law said, "He ain't nothin' but gutter dirt. You wanna know where he is? I'll tell you where he is. He's laid up in a hotel with some scarlet woman."

Helen said, "But I love him."

Lardo's mother said, "Why, I can't understand. This isn't like my Lardo. I bet he's sick. Yes, sir! Truth be known, my Lardo has got magnesia, lost his memory. Dear God! My baby's got magnesia."

Lardo's daddy said, "In the name of God, woman. It ain't magnesia, it's amnesia. But that ain't what's wrong with that boy, Mama. You know he's my own flesh and blood and I love him just as much as I would if he had good sense, but there's something we must face, as unpleasant as it is. Our son, Lardo, was born a dodo. He has lived a dodo, and, God forgive him, in all likelihood he will die a dodo."

While all this was going on, our hero was on a Greyhound bus, wearing red cowboy boots, headed for Music City, U.S.A.

Once in Nashville, he took a furnished apartment. He unpacked and hung up all his old show-business clothes, sequins intact.

Lardo knew that in a matter of days, Nashville would be at his feet. His fantasies knew no bounds. He would have a monster hit record, then another, then another, sold-out concerts from coast to coast. The world's first billion-seller album.

He even thought about the title of the best-selling album. He spent hours trying to come up with the right one. Lardo knew if he was going to have a billion-seller album, the title was very important. His imagination ran wild. How about "Lardo Sings His Guts Out"? No, that was not sophisticated enough. How about "Lardo Sings His Ass Off"? No, that wouldn't do either. Then it came to him. He would call it "Lardo Live at the Great Pyramid." He could see it now. There he was standing on top of the Great Pyramid, one spotlight trained on him, far below 200,000 Egyptians, applauding, scream-ing and throwing their turbans in the air, chanting over and over, "Lardo, Lardo, Lardo."

He would make movies with Burt Reynolds, TV spe-cials with Dolly Parton. He would open his own amusement park and call it "Lardo Land."

He would do the Carson Show. He would buy a house next door to Johnny Cash. It would be so big that you could hold a dove hunt indoors. He would have a huge swimming pool in the shape of a sequin.

Yes, sir, Lardo's fantasy knew no bounds. Unfortunately, his talent knew many bounds.

He haunted every place in Nashville that might listen to one of his songs. He was able to make ends meet by playing at small clubs at night and working at 7-11 in the daytime.

The first six months he was in Nashville he lived almost entirely on hope. He spent over a week's salary from the 7-11 to get a demo record made. He went to every radio station within fifty miles trying to get it played. Everybody told him the same thing — nice title but the song won't sell, and the way you do it leaves a lot to be desired.

On more than one occasion, Lardo thought about giving up and going home, but he knew deep down inside his chubby, little heart that he would rather die a horrible death than to go home a failure for a second time.

He knew that's what they all expected, and what's more important, with the exception of his sainted mother, he knew that's what they all wanted.

His second six months were worse than the first. The hope he had lived on was gone, and one lonely morning Lardo was forced to face one inescapable fact: He was never going to make it in Nashville as a singer/songwriter. He was tired of walking the sidewalks. He was tired of the rejection and, most of all, he was tired of feeling like a failure.

The only thing Lardo wanted to do was to give up, but he wasn't sure how. He had already decided he couldn't go home, and he didn't know where to go in Nashville to surrender.

For days on end he pondered his lot in life, suffering the pain of rejection that had become synonymous with Nashville. Finally he decided there was only one way out. He reasoned that if he couldn't manage his life, he could sure manage his death. Lardo decided the solution to his problem was to kill himself.

Once the decision was made, the only thing left to decide was how the foul deed was to be done. He ruled out a gun because he didn't own one and, considering the current shape of his finances, if he had a pistol, he wouldn't be able to afford a bullet.

Cutting his wrist was also out of the question. Lardo was squeamish by nature, and there was no way that he could take a razor blade and cut his wrist. The thought of dying didn't bother him much, but he found the thought of pain to be a definite turn-off.

He could crash his car into a bridge abutment. Only one problem here — he didn't own a car. And he knew it would be almost impossible to get a Nashville taxi driver to drive into a bridge abutment.

He thought about jumping in the river, but his experiences in the Hudson River had convinced him that he didn't want to kill himself by drowning.

There seemed to be only one option left open to him — he would hang himself. That was it, he was going to hold a necktie party, and he would be the guest of honor.

He was delighted that it was payday at the 7-11, 'cause he knew that if he were going to kill himself, it would take some money to do it right.

He went from the 7-11 to the hardware store and purchased twenty feet of very soft rope. He stopped by the whiskey store and bought a quart of Jack Daniels. Then he walked back to his room.

Once inside, he said to himself, "I've been in Nashville all these months and today is the first time anything seems to be going right."

He dressed in his best sequined outfit, pulled on his red cowboy boots, and sat down to write a suicide note. Unfortunately, Lardo was no better at writing suicide notes than he was at writing songs.

The note said:

To whom it may concern: By the time you read this, I will be pickin' and singin' with Jesus.

Have a nice day,

Lardo.

He left the note on the table, walked outside, and caught a cab.

The driver said, "Where to, cowboy?"

Lardo said, "Just take me out of town about twenty dollars worth."

The taxi was soon out of town and roaring through the beautiful Tennessee countryside.

When they were well out into the country, Lardo said to the driver, "Anywhere along here will be all right."

He stood beside the road holding the sack containing the rope and the Jack Daniels and watched the taxi until it was out of sight.

He walked off across a big grassy field. All he needed to find was a private place with a tree and he was in business, or, in his case, out of business.

He walked for about ten minutes and finally came to the top of a hill.

A beautiful meadow lay at the bottom, and there was a small lake and, most important, a lot of trees that would be perfect for a hanging.

He walked around the lake until he found what he considered to be the perfect tree. He was so busy looking for a spot to die that he didn't even notice the old man fishing at one end of the lake. The old man had watched Lardo come down the hill and walk from tree to tree. He was watching Lardo's every move, but Lardo never even knew he was there.

Lardo sat down under the big shade tree and took the rope and the Jack Daniels out of the sack.

The old man watched in stony-faced silence.

Lardo opened the Jack Daniels, held the bottle up as if he was making a toast, and said to himself, "For once in my life, I'm going to get drunker than a four-eyed goat and never worry about a hangover."

He sat there for about twenty minutes drinking and staring into space.

When he felt that he had consumed enough courage, he stood up, put the top back on the bottle and placed it carefully on the ground at the base of the tree.

He started to climb the tree and mumbled to himself, "I hope I'm not too drunk to climb this old tree and hang myself, 'cause if I don't it's going to ruin my whole day."

Even in his whiskey-logged brain, he was able to reason that if his rope was twenty feet long he needed to be at least thirty feet up in the tree to make this suicide a proper one.

He finally made it to a large limb that he judged was about thirty feet off the ground. To be sure, he lowered the rope, and sure enough, the end swung back and forth about ten feet from Mother Earth.

Lardo took great pains tying the rope to the limb.

Then he thought, I hope a songwriter finds my body. He could write a great song about me and perhaps I could be famous in death. It ain't much, but it's better than dying a 7-11 employee.

It was time. Lardo wanted to get this over with before he sobered up.

He sat very straight on the big limb, looked up briefly, shouted in a loud voice, "I'm comin', Jesus!" and hurled himself out of the top of that great tree.

It would have been one of the world's truly great suicides except for one thing: Lardo was so drunk that he had neglected to tie the rope around his neck.

While he was falling, he waited for that sudden snap that would start his journey to Glory, but of course it never came.

He hit the ground on his back with a loud thud that seemed to shake the entire meadow. Lying there with his eyes closed, he thought, Am I dead? If I am, it sure hurts like hell to die.

He opened his eyes and saw the old man standing over him, staring down.

Lardo looked up at the old man for a long time. Finally the old man spoke. "Boy," he said, "you don't know nothing about killin' yourself, do ya?"

Lardo asked, "Are you Jesus?"

The old man said, "Naw, I'm Eugene. You want me to help you back up the tree?"

"No, I appreciate it, but I guess I'm kinda out of the mood."

The old man said, "What's them shiny things all over the ground?"

"They're sequins," said Lardo. "I guess I jarred them off my suit when I hit the ground."

The old man said, "Can I help you up, Lardo?"

Surprised, Lardo said, "How did you know my name?"

"Saw it wrote on the back of your suit when you was climbing the tree. How come you dress so funny?"

"'Cause I'm in show business."

"You sure you don't want me to help you back up the tree?"

"No thanks. Maybe later," Lardo said.

The old man said, "I got a string of fish down in the lake that I'm fixin' to cook up. You'd be welcome to supper."

"Well, I did kind of work up an appetite climbing that tree, and Lord knows, my social calendar is clear.

Yes, sir, I sure will have a bite with you, if you're sure it's no trouble."

"No trouble at all. Bring that bottle of Jack Daniels with you. It'll go mighty good with supper. If you want me to, I'll help you get your rope out of the tree after we eat."

"Naw," Lardo said, "I think I'll just leave it up there."

During supper, Lardo told the old man his story. He talked nonstop. He started with the first guitar lesson and told him every detail. He told about the Ted Mack show, about his dip in the Hudson River, his marriage, his job.

He told about running away to Nashville and what a failure he had been. He poured out his heart about being too ashamed to go back home.

When he had finished, he said, "Eugene, you're older and wiser than me. Where did I go wrong?"

The old man took another pull on the Jack Daniels and said, "Well, it seems to me that your worst mistake was forgetting to tie that rope around your neck."

Lardo was shocked and his voice showed it.

"Eugene," he said, "I can't believe what you're sayin'. Do you really think my suicide was a good idea?"

The old man said, "Well, Lardo, I ain't knowed you long, and I ain't had a lot of time to study on it, but from what you told me, I think your suicide was a dandy little idea.

"Look at it this way, my boy — you got no choice. You can't stay in Nashville, 'cause you ain't got no talent, and you're too yellow to go back home and face the music. Yes sir, you were right in the first place. If anybody would be better off dead, it's you, Lardo."

Lardo said, "I can't believe what I'm hearin'. People are supposed to talk you out of killin' yourself, not recommend it."

The old man said, "Lardo, you got to have more faith in your own judgment. You ain't much, Lardo, but when you're right, you're right. Now get up from there and go on up yonder and hang yourself. You take my word for it, it's the only way out."

Lardo was angry now. He shouted, "You're sick in the head, old man."

Eugene took another long pull on the bottle and said, "Let's examine the facts here. You're out in the middle of Gawd knows where, wearing funny clothes with them shiny things all over you, wearing red boots, jumpin' out of the top of trees trying to kill yourself, and you think I'm crazy! Face it, Lardo, you're a failure and a dumb ass to boot!"

"Failure, am I?" said Lardo. "I'll show you who's a failure. You know what I'm gonna do? I'm going back to Nashville and become a success in show business."

Lardo spun on his heels and started walking back up the hill toward the highway.

When he was out of earshot, the old man chuckled softly and said, "Atta boy, Lardo, you ain't never beat 'til you quit."

Lardo caught a ride back to Nashville, and for the first time in weeks he got a good night's sleep.

The next morning he was on the street bright and early.

He was on his way to his job at the 7-11, but he was not going to work. He was going to quit. He passed a sign that said Pyramid Music Company. He stopped dead in his tracks. The logo on the sign had a man with a guitar standing on top of the Great Pyramid.

Lardo said, "It's a sign, it's a sign from heaven. God wants me to go in and audition my songs for these wonderful people."

He went in, caught the elevator, and got off on the second floor. Straight ahead was a wooden door with a glass inset. The inset also had the pyramid logo on it. Deep down in his heart old Lardo knew that going through that door would change his whole life.

He was surprised when he got inside. He had expected to see a giant lobby with row after row of mahogany doors leading to private offices and employees busily running around making people famous.

Instead, he found one room with a bald-headed man in a seersucker suit sitting behind a desk. The desk was full of papers and it looked like they had not been touched since Andrew Jackson left Nashville.

The bald-headed man said, "What can I do for you?"

Lardo said, "I'm a songwriter."

"I know that. Now what can I do for you?"

"How did you know I was a songwriter?" Lardo said.

Looking bored, the bald-headed man said, "The sequined musical notes on your shirt were my first clue, and not many brain surgeons carry guitar cases."

Lardo made his pitch, played two songs, and asked the bald-headed man for his opinion.

The man sat back in his chair, took a long drag on a cigar and said, "Well, I'll tell you, my boy. I didn't like the song much, and you can't sing at all. Let me give you a little piece of show business advice. In Nashville, Tennessee, songwriters are a dime a dozen. As a matter of fact, most people in Nashville are here because they think they can write country-and-western songs. And you want to know something else? Most of them can. That is to say, once you come up with a title, any fool can write a song. Writing song titles and selling 'em to these yahoos is where the money is."

Lardo said, "Hold on a minute. Are you tellin' me that a man can make a living just writin' titles for songs?"

"Yes, sir," the bald-headed man replied. "And plenty of money if he happens to have the gift of title-writin'. Tell you what, son. Bring me some titles and I'll give you fifty dollars for every one I think is good enough to sell."

Lardo knew he could do it. He was up most of the night writing titles, and, as they say, the rest is history.

Lardo now has his own song-title business, and some of the biggest names in country music buy their titles from Lardo.

His first big hit was one called "The Horse You Rode in On."

He also wrote "The McCullough Lightweight Blues."

A few of his bigger hits are "So's Yo' Mama," "If My Mule Looked Like You I'd Leave Him in the Barn," "I'd Marry My Truck, But It Ain't Legal," "Lookin' at You Makes Me Slobber," "I'd Marry Your Dog Just to Get in the Family," "Too Much Beer Makes My Mama Sweat" and "My First Husband Was a Polish Joke."

The money and the hits kept on comin'.

Lardo sent for his family. They came to Nashville and, as they say in the fairy tales, "lived happily ever after."

— from —
WHO CARES ABOUT APATHY? (1987)

PROFESSIONAL GOSSIP

Gossip can be an ugly thing. It has ruined lives, toppled empires and spoiled marriages. Gossip, however, can be fun if it's handled by experts.

We had two such experts in my hometown, Miss Lucille and Miss Emma. These two ladies had devoted a lifetime to polishing their gossip skills and countless years sharpening their tongues to a razor-like sharpness. They held their sessions on Miss Emma's screened-in front porch. Both ladies were doing needlepoint while seated in large, white rocking chairs. There were no rules once the gossip started. They would say anything about anybody. It was free-style, take-no-prisoners gossip. It usually sounded something like this:

"Poor old Mrs. Ross — those kids of hers are driving her to an early grave."

"Ain't that the truth. Just goes to show, they're more trouble and heartaches when they're grown than they were as babies."

"What's Charles doing?"

"Lord only knows. He ain't drawed three sober breaths in a row since he got back from the Army."

"Does he work?"

"Lord God knows, you cain't work if you're too drunk to stand up. He was a house painter for a while, but got fired when his boss found the liquor he hid in the commode tank. His wife left him, you know. Poor thing … I guess she just couldn't take no more."

"Where is he now?"

"Lord only knows. Last thing I heard, he was down in Macon laid up with a woman. It's a wonder his mama ain't slap gray headed with worry."

"Have you met the new preacher?"

"Not only that, I met his bottle-blonde wife."

"Does she bleach her hair?"

"You just look at those black roots and make up your own mind."

"Did you like her?"

"Oh, she's all right, but she don't act much like a preacher's wife. You know what I think? I think if she had the chance, she'd gossip."

"You don't mean it, not the preacher's wife."

"I sure do mean it."

"If there's one thing on God's earth I can't stand, it's a gossip."

"Ain't that the Lord's truth."

"Did you hear about Ruth Whitlock leaving her husband?"

THE BALLAD OF BONEY AND CLAUDE

I went to high school with a lot of out-and-out characters. My class reunions are always something to behold. The real fun of a class reunion is discovering how everybody turns out.

The treasurer of our senior class was an old girl named Ima Jean Bailey. She was about five-foot-ten, and after a big meal she weighed about ninety pounds. She was so skinny that she could get into a T-shirt from either end. We all had nicknames in high school, and poor old skinny Ima Jean became known to one and all as "Boney." It didn't take long before even the teachers were calling her "Boney." She never openly admitted it, but I always thought she took some pride in her nickname. She was a bright girl with a lot of personality, and everybody in school knew and liked her.

The captain of our football team was our full-back, Claude Williams. He was a mountain of a lad, about six foot three inches tall and weighed 265. Claude was older than the rest of us because he had failed three years on his way to being a senior in high school. The standard joke was that Claude was the only student in our school who could vote. Claude didn't seem to mind the joke. It was not that he was good-natured, it was just that he didn't understand it. Claude would play football and that was about it. He was the only person I ever knew who failed music appreciation. The point

I'm trying to make is that, above all else, Claude was dumb. Nice, but dumb.

Midway through our senior year, Ima Jean and Claude fell madly, passionately in love. And thus began "The ballad of Boney and Claude."

Shortly after we graduated, Claude joined the Army. He was discharged three years later with one stripe and a tattoo that said "Ima Jean" under a red rose.

Claude went to plumber's school on the G.I. Bill. The day he graduated, Boney and Claude were married. He was thirty minutes late getting to his own wedding; seems he couldn't remember which church to go to. When the minister asked Claude, "Do you take this woman to be your lawfully wedded wife?" Claude said, "Yeah." There was low laughter in the church, but as soon as Boney punched him in the ribs with her elbow, he said, "Boy! Howdy, I sure do."

As we left the church, we were all sure that they would live happily ever after. It was more than obvious that they were very much in love. You could see it in her eyes, and I don't guess you have a girl's name tattooed on your arm if you don't really love her.

The years were not kind to the love birds. Claude bounced from one job to another. He was a hard, willing worker, but since he had the IQ of a lug wrench, it was very hard for him to hold a job for very long.

One night, while they were watching an *Ironsides* rerun on their rented TV, Boney said, "Claude, I think I have figured out a way that we can get out of debt."

In his usual alert manner, Claude said, "Huh?"

Boney told him that they were going to rob a bank.

Claude said, "What if we get caught?"

Boney explained that if they went to a small, country bank and waited until it was almost empty of customers, there would be little or no risk.

"We ain't even got a gun and no money to buy one," Claude said.

"We don't need a real gun. I saw a water pistol in the dime store the other day, and it looks exactly like a .45 automatic. Nobody on earth can tell it from a real gun."

Claude said, "Yeah, and if somebody tries to stop us, we'll drown 'em."

"Don't worry, Honey," Boney said, "I'll explain exactly how to do it."

The next day, they went to the dime store and bought the water pistol. Claude played with the gun while Boney checked the map for a small town that had a bank. When they found just the right size town, they drove there in Claude's pick-up to check it out. Everything seemed perfect. The town was so small it only had one policeman. It also held the one and only branch of the Farmers and Merchants Bank of Ritter County.

Boney and Claude watched the bank all that day. There was only one teller and the manager. Most of the time there were no customers at all. Boney made a mental note. The manager went to lunch at twelve o'clock, leaving the elderly woman teller alone in the bank. It seemed like the perfect bank for two trainee robbers to start with.

That night, Boney wrote a note that said, "Put all

your money in this sack and nobody will get hurt." She then made Claude put down his comic book while she explained to him what his job would be the next day. She spoke slowly and gave detailed instructions.

"Claude, here is all you have to do. We wait until the manager goes to lunch and the teller is alone. I'll wait in the truck with the motor running. All you have to do, Claude, is go into the bank, hand the lady the note and the sack, and show her the gun. She will fill the sack full of money, and you walk out of the bank very calmly, and then we drive off. Believe me, Claude," she went on, "nothing can go wrong if you do exactly as I tell you. This is foolproof."

Claude smiled and said, "It'll be like takin' candy away from someone fallin' off a log."

The next day they got up and dressed. Boney went over the plan three more times to make sure Claude had it clearly in mind. They stopped on the way out of town and filled the pick-up with gas. The sun was shining and it seemed like a perfect day to "go into business for yourself," as Boney said.

They got to the front of the bank right on time. It was five minutes till twelve, and there were no customers in the bank. The noon news came on the truck radio, and right on cue, the manager walked out of the bank, got in his car, and drove away.

Boney said, "O.K., Claude, do you have the note?"
"Yep!"
"Do you have the sack?"
"Yep!"

"Do you have the gun?"

"Yep!"

"Do you remember what to do?"

Claude said, "Dawg gone, Boney, sometimes you treat me like I ain't got no sense at all. Don't you remember I graduated twelfth in my class from plumbing school?"

Boney said, "Claude, you ain't going in there to unstop a commode, you're going in there to rob 'em. Besides, there were only ten people in your class."

They kissed and Claude got out of the truck and strolled into the bank. He walked up to the teller's window, as cool as the center seed of a cucumber. The elderly lady smiled and said, "Can I help you, young man?"

Claude smiled back and said, "Yes, ma'am. I got a note here for you from my wife."

She read the note and said, "You wouldn't want to shoot me, now would you, my boy?"

Claude paused and said, "I wouldn't mind." She started to fill the sack with loose bills.

Outside, Boney's heart nearly stopped when the town's only police car pulled up beside her, stopped, and the policeman got out and walked into the bank. Claude did not see him come in.

The officer sized up the situation immediately. In a loud, commanding voice, he said, "What's going on here?" With no hesitation at all, Claude spun around and squirted the policeman right between the eyes with his water pistol.

Boney and Claude were not at our last class reunion, but I bet their ears were burning.

THE ULTIMATE BARBECUE JOINT

I hope, by now, that most people realize I am one of the world's foremost authorities on barbecue. Goodness knows, I've told them enough times. I have eaten good "Q" all over the South. I've eaten it in Mom & Pop joints and in the big, franchised places.

One time, when I was desperate, I even ate beef barbecue.

After all these years of testing, re-testing, learning and experimenting, I have decided to take the big plunge and open up the world's first perfect barbecue joint.

A barbecue joint is much more than just good barbecue. There are actually dozens of elements that go into the "perfect" place.

In my travels in rural north Georgia, I have discovered the perfect, and I mean the perfect, location. On a recent Sunday outing with the family, we found an old, vacant, red brick church. It's not big, but it's big enough. It still has the stained glass windows and it will give me just the right atmosphere for my barbecue joint. It goes without saying, of course, that the name is important. The name of my place will be "The Que, Stew and Pew."

The menu will be simple but will satisfy the tastes of any true Southern barbecue lover:

1. We will serve pork only. Research clearly shows that people who eat beef barbecue also like tongue, liver, and broccoli and carry pictures of commies in

their wallets. The pork would be either sliced or chopped, since we are trying to please the masses.

2. Our Brunswick stew will be made in a gigantic, black pot, and it will be stirred from time to time with a sawed-off canoe paddle. It will contain only the wonderful things that the good Lord decreed should go into real Brunswick stew. That means no English peas.

3. We will serve white loaf bread. Our bread will be the freshest available anywhere. We will serve it fresh from the sack or toasted over the same grill that the meat was cooked on.

4. Our fourth and final food item will be potato chips. Not the kind with ridges, not the kind that is flavored with garlic or onion or barbecue, just plain old honest-to-goodness fresh, wonderful potato chips.

These will be the only food items sold. If somebody comes in and wants a cheeseburger, we will direct him to the nearest drive-in window at the Burger Doodle.

If someone comes in and wants barbecue beef, the waitresses will all laugh and the cook will holler things about his Mama until he leaves.

Like the food menu, the drink menu will be simple, yet elegant. We will serve sweet iced tea in large, large glasses. This will be brought to your table by the waitress. If a customer does not want iced tea, we will offer soft drinks. They, however, will not be brought to your table. They will be self-service and kept in a large drink box full of ice cold water. The soft drinks, of course, will be in bottles only; to serve one in a can would seriously affect the type of atmosphere that we are trying to create. We will serve Coca-Cola, Pepsi, R.C. Cola and both orange and grape Nehi.

In a true Southern barbecue joint, the employees are very important. We will have three waitresses: Roxy, Dixie and Jolean.

The cashier will double as the cook during the rush hours. His name will be Eugene Lamar, and he will keep a kitchen match dangling from the corner of his mouth at all times. If we cannot hire someone named Eugene Lamar, then we will hire someone with initials for a first name like J. W. or W. D.

The Que, Stew and Pew will be open only on Friday, Saturday and Sunday. I will need the other four days to make bank deposits and get ready for the weekend rush. I will put an ad in the paper as soon as I open, so you can come to the world's only perfect barbecue joint.

In the meantime, if you run into anybody named Eugene Lamar, would you ask him to call me?

IT STILL BEATS ME

I long ago decided that there are some things in life that I am not supposed to understand. I don't mean the big things, like how to make a trip to the moon or algebra. I mean simple, everyday things that I should be able to figure out but, for the life of me, can't. Let me give you a few examples.

Every time we have a big election in this country, the newspapers are full of stories about the huge campaign debts of the losers. The next thing we hear is that somebody is giving a big fund-raising dinner for the fellow who went into debt while losing an election.

Now, that's a good and proper thing to do, and I have no problem whatsoever with it. My question is this: Why do we never hear about a benefit to pay off the winner's debts? It obviously costs as much, if not more, to win an election than it does to lose one. So how does the poor winner pay his debts? That could be a question we're better off not knowing the answer to.

I have never understood prom parties. Do you remember how they were? You stood around and drank punch that you didn't like, trying to display manners that you didn't have. When you were ready to throw up from too much punch, you got to take a girl on a prom. That meant a walk around the block. Nothing happened, you just walked around the block. I went to many prom parties in my time, but I don't know why I kept going back, because your average prom party is about as much fun as unloading a dishwasher.

Why do airlines say they had a "near miss" when we all know what they actually had was a "near hit"?

Why do newspapers say that somebody in a wreck "barely escaped death?" They never say when someone is killed that they failed to escape death, or had a tie with death.

Why do Hershey's with almonds cost the same as Hershey bars with no almonds?

Why do traffic reporters refer to all streets other than expressways as surface streets? I thought, except for a few tunnels, all streets were on the surface.

Why does the highway department put up signs that say, "Bridge may ice in winter?" Seems to me that most folks know that dang near everything may ice in winter.

Why do radio stations say they are going to play ten "hits" in a row, and then come in after every record to assure you that you are hearing ten hits in a row? Then they give the station call letters, the time, the temperature and where your dial is set before they go back to the music.

Why do you need a license to fish, but you don't have to have one to drink whiskey?

Why do they call a glove compartment a glove compartment?

Why do people at drive-in windows tell you to "Drive around please"? Do they think you're going to wait there for your food?

What is in McDonald's special sauce, and when are they going to McShut up about it?

Why do football coaches always refer to themselves

as "we"? "We are expecting big things for our boys." "We try to develop men." "We enjoy coaching." Makes you wonder if they're pregnant, doesn't it?

Yes sir, there are a lot of things that I'm still trying to figure out.

THE TRUTH ABOUT APATHY

My uncle, Seth Porch, was the happiest man I ever knew. I don't ever remember seeing him when he wasn't smiling. He was even tempered, loving, and managed to get through life by never sweating the small stuff.

In the middle 1930s, Uncle Seth was approached by some local men who wanted him to join the Ku Klux Klan. Seth said, "Why would I want to join the Klan? I'm already an Elk and a Mason, and that's about enough meetings for anyone to attend."

One of the men said, "But don't you want to keep the blacks from taking over?"

Seth laughed and said, "Takin' over? Most blacks I know are having about as hard a time as I am makin' ends meet. Besides, if I leave them alone, they're gonna leave me alone, and whatever they decide to do is none of my business."

When the war in Vietnam was in full swing, somebody asked Seth what he thought about our involvement. Seth scratched his head and said, "I don't know too much about it, but it seems like a right long way to go to mind somebody else's business."

The board of deacons at Seth's church once called a special meeting to discuss the length of the new pastor's wife's skirts. She was not wearing mini skirts by any means, but some of the ladies of the congregation felt that decent women had to wear their skirts a certain length, and they agreed that the pastor's wife must set the "proper" example.

Seth let all the other deacons talk, and when it was his turn, he stood up and said, "The pastor is a good man; he works hard for dang little money. I figure the way his wife dresses is her business and not mine. Now, I suggest we adjourn, go home, watch Perry Mason, and, from now on, try to mind our own business."

The dictionary defines apathy as (1) lack of emotion or feeling; (2) lack of interest in things generally found exciting, interesting or moving; indifference.

Uncle Seth defined it as minding your own business.

I'm with Uncle Seth.

— from —

JONAS WILKERSON WAS A GRAVY-SUCKIN' PIG (1988)

SUPER STUMPERS

If you can answer any ten of the following twenty-five questions, you get your Ph.D. in trivia.

SUPER STUMPER QUESTIONS

1. Name the military academy featured in the 1981 movie *Taps.*
2. Who created Coca-Cola?
3. What is Donald Duck's automobile tag number?
4. Who is Ramon Estevez?
5. What was the name of the nun in the 1957 movie *Heaven Knows Mr. Allison*?
6. Who played the part of the killer in the movie *Dial M for Murder*?
7. Name singer Johnnie Ray's only movie.
8. Name the saloon where John Wayne was killed in *The Shootist.*

9. What was Mrs. Miniver's first name?
10. What was singer Gene Austin's theme song?
11. Who was Nancy Drew's adopted mother?
12. Can you name Marcus Welby's boat?
13. What TV character was from Mill Valley, California?
14. Name Ma and Pa Kettle's horse.
15. What was President Grant's favorite drink?
16. On *The Mary Tyler Moore Show*, what was Mary's father's occupation?
17. Who was the first winner of the Cy Young award?
18. Who was Paul Bunyan's son?
19. Name Judge Roy Bean's saloon.
20. Who was Buz Sawyer's best friend?
21. What was Secret Agent X-9's real identity?
22. Who was the policeman buddy of Philo Vance?
23. Name the U.S. Coast Guard song.
24. Who was the third child of Adam and Eve?
25. What tennis player has won more Wimbledon titles than anyone else?

SUPER STUMPER ANSWERS

1. Bunker Hill
2. Dr. John S. Pemberton
3. 313
4. Real name of actor Martin Sheen
5. Sister Angela
6. Grace Kelly
7. *There's No Business Like Show Business* (1954)
8. The Acme Saloon
9. Kay
10. "My Blue Heaven"
11. Mrs. Hannah Gruen
12. *The Mary D.*
13. B. J. Hunnicutt on *M*A*S*H*
14. Emma
15. Old Crow
16. Doctor
17. Don Newcombe in 1956
18. Jean
19. The Jersey Lily
20. Roscoe Sweeney
21. He was known only as Mr. Corrigan.
22. Sergeant Ernest Heath
23. "Semper Paratus"
24. Seth
25. Billie Jean King

— from —

HONEST, OFFICER, THE MIDGET WAS ON FIRE WHEN I GOT HERE (1989)

TALK SHOW

I am one of the luckiest men on the face of the earth. I have been allowed, for most of my adult life, to earn a living doing something that many people would do for free. I have my own talk radio show.

I have never known anyone who was ever in radio that has been completely happy doing anything else. I know doctors, lawyers and professional jocks who would trade jobs with me in a heartbeat.

I'm not sure why it's such a fun job. I do know that when I'm on the air, the hours fly by, and I am on a high that few, if any other, jobs can equal.

I'm not saying it's not a high-pressure job. Lord knows, it is! I have seen some very talented talk-show hosts fired because of one bad rating book. I have worked for some program directors who couldn't find their own fanny in a phone booth. And I have come to accept that in radio, like TV, the least creative people are always in charge of creativity.

With all of its drawbacks, however, it is still the world's best job.

It's my world, and, God, how I do love it!

THE DUMP BUTTON

To do live talk radio, it is necessary to operate on a delay system. This simply means that the audience hears what has been said six seconds later than it was actually spoken.

In the event a caller says something that is not suitable for the public airways, the host has six seconds to hit the "dump button" and delete the objectionable comment.

Some of the funniest things ever said on radio never are heard outside the booth because the host or producer was able to cut them out.

I will never forget the time when my topic was, "What is the government doing for you that you want them to stop?"

The lines were full of people making very serious comments about the government sticking its nose into their lives.

I put a caller on the line, and, in a very serious voice, he said, "Ludlow, the Navy must be made to stop putting saltpeter into our sailors' food."

Like the unsuspecting clown I was, I asked, "Why?"

He said, "Because they gave me some in 1943, and it's just now starting to work."

I hit the "dump button" and moved on to the next call. The lady on the line was laughing her head off. I said, "What are you laughing at?"

She said, "I think I know that guy."

I have one nut who has been calling me about once a week for ten years. When I answer the phone, all he says is, "Do-do." I, of course, hit the "dump button" and immediately hang up on him.

This must be the most determined pervert on the face of the earth because the next week he calls back with the same routine. He does not seem to mind that for ten years he has been trying to say "do-do" on the radio, and, to date, nobody in radioland has ever even heard his voice.

I have considered letting him say it and get it out of his twisted little system. I decided, however, to continue to dump him, since, as a talk-show host, I hate to lose a regular caller.

I had a guest on several years ago to discuss a play he had written that was a big hit. To say my guest was a little light in the loafers was giving him the benefit of every doubt. The fact of the matter is that this old boy was much, much more feminine than Audrey Hepburn.

He did not seem to be interested in talking about his play, but, rather, preferred to talk about "gay rights." Every time I would ask a question about the play, his answer would have something to do with the fact that he was gay and proud of it. When I started taking calls, the callers were quick to condemn his lifestyle, and he was just as quick to call them close-minded bigots.

Finally, an elderly lady called and started out her comment by saying, "I am a Christian." I have learned, over the years, that means the caller is about to say something very un-Christian. This call was no exception.

You could feel the hate in her voice as she started to lecture my guest. I said, "Ma'am, you said you were a Christian, but it sounds to me like you hate this man."

She shouted back, "I don't hate anybody, but this man should be down on his knees praying."

In a high-pitched, quivering voice, my guest shot back, "Lady, when I get on my knees, I've got better things to do than pray!"

Thank God for that wonderful little "dump button."

There have been two occasions when I had to hit the "dump button" on myself. (There have been about two thousand occasions when I should have and didn't.)

Skip Caray, the very talented voice of the Atlanta Braves, dedicated his life, for awhile, to breaking me up on the air. In the late 1970s, Skip and I worked together at the old Ring Radio, WRNG in Atlanta. One of our sponsors was the Honeybaked Ham Company.

In those days, all of the Honeybaked Ham spots were read live. The last line in the commercial read, "Honeybaked — the ham so good it will haunt you till it's gone." We had been given instructions to read that last line with a great deal of feeling and sincerity.

I was reading the spot one day when Skip came silently into the broadcast booth behind me. I didn't hear him, and I had no idea he was there. When I came to the all-important last line in the commercial, Skip gave me a big, wet kiss in the ear. I probably could have handled that, but when his lips were about a quarter-inch away from my ear, static electricity arched between us. I got a sharp shock in my ear, followed by a big, wet kiss. This is the way the commercial ended: "Honeybaked — the ham so good it will — JESUS CHRIST!"

People called the front desk for two hours asking why we had bleeped our own commercial. We never told a soul — until now.

We had a news anchor at Ring Radio named Brenda. In addition to being a very talented news person, Brenda had been richly blessed by Mother Nature. She was very well built and did more for a sweater than Izod. As I was on the air one day, I looked up and saw the shapely Brenda outside the studio, looking through the glass, eating a very large and juicy pear.

Without thinking twice, I said into the open mike, "Brenda has the biggest pear I have ever seen."

It was an innocent remark, and I did not realize I had said anything wrong until Brenda spit pear juice all over the glass window and my producer fell out of his chair. Fortunately, he hit the "dump button" before he lost consciousness.

NAUGHTY TALK

I do a thing on the air every once in awhile that I call "Letters to Ludlow." It works a little like "Dear Abby," except that Abby gets real letters, and I make mine up.

I just write myself a letter, sign a phony name to it, read it on the air and ask my audience for their comments. No matter how off the wall I make my letters, I always get very interesting calls.

I read the following letter on the air:

Dear Ludlow:

I just read in the local paper that the federal government is about to give $2.5 million to promote theater arts in our area. I have checked into this, and frankly, I am outraged.

A recent survey has shown that over ninety percent of the people in our area involved in the theater are known to be practicing thespians. Ludlow, this is a disgrace. I don't care what these wretched creatures do in the privacy of their own homes, but to use tax money is going absolutely too far!

Please let your radio audience know that our tax money is being used on thespians.

Just sign me...
Outraged in Oakland City

I read the letter on the air and watched the phones light up. I have always been amazed at the number of people who will call a talk show and try to make a comment when they are not real sure what we are talking about.

One of the first calls I received was from a lady who said, "We should try and be more tolerant of thespians. After all, they can't help it. They are born that way."

Another woman called and said there were many new treatments nowadays and that psychiatrists were having great success treating thespians.

She closed her conversation by saying, "With medical science being what it is today, you don't have to be a thespian if you don't want to be."

One man, who had figured out what I was up to, called to get in on the fun. He said, in a very serious tone of voice, "I have it on very good authority that John Wayne was a practicing thespian for well over fifty years."

I shot right back, "Hold on a second, Buster. John Wayne was a great American. John Wayne was a credit to his mama and daddy. And if you think I'm going to sit here and listen to you besmirch the Duke's good name, you are out of your evil mind!" Then I hung up on him.

In the course of the next two hours, I talked to about twenty-five people who had no idea what a thespian was but nevertheless wanted to talk about our topic.

I think there is a lesson to be learned here, and it was summed up by the call our general manager received from one irate lady. She said, "I don't know what it means, but I know you shouldn't be talking about it on the radio."

THE ELEPHANT

Some days nothing seems to go right for you on the radio. Just when you think you are so bright and so sophisticated, somebody is going to come along and bring you back down to earth.

About halfway through the show, a man called and said, "Ludlow, I have a riddle for you."

I said, "O.K., Partner. Let's have it."

He said, "Can you tell me what is gray and comes in quarts?"

I say, "Boy, that's tough. Let me see — What is gray and comes in quarts? What could it be — gray and comes in quarts."

I could hear the guy starting to giggle softly on the phone.

I finally said, "I give up. You're going to have to tell me. What is gray and comes in quarts?"

He said, "You really don't know?"

And I said it again — "No, I don't know what is gray and comes in quarts."

The guy said, "Elephants."

I said, "I don't get it. Elephants don't come in quarts."

By this time he was laughing his head off. He said, "Wanna bet?"

It finally hit me. It was too late to bleep out what he had said.

It took me about two years to live that one down.

HOMER SOUTHWELL

Another of my exciting radio spoofs was Homer Southwell.

The idea for Homer came to me in the middle of the night. I got out of bed, found my briefcase, went to my dining room table, and Homer Southwell was born.

I thought it would be funny to have a guest on the air who was such a bigot that he hated, loathed and despised anything or anyone from the North.

I wanted him to be such a dirty, disgusting, no good S.O.B. that even his mother would short-sheet him if she had a chance.

Sitting at my dining room table, I decided I needed an excuse to have him on the radio, so I made him an author who was in Atlanta on a book tour.

His first book was called *Yankee, Go Home*. He had also written a sequel called *And Stay There*.

I worked most of the night coming up with venomous lines for Homer to say — lines that would make people so mad they would call and rip all the bark off of old Homer. Some of his original lines were:

1. The best form of birth control known to mankind is a Bronx accent.

2. For entertainment, Homer said he read the *New York Times* obit column.

3. Santa Claus did not go to see the children up north.

4. Yankee women did not shave their legs.

When I had all the material put together, all I needed was to find someone to play the part of Homer

Southwell.

The next day I still had not decided who would be my Homer. My phone rang, and as soon as I heard the voice on the other end of the line, I knew who Homer was going to be. On the phone from Chicago was my stepbrother, Lewis Grizzard.

Lewis told me he was coming home for the Christmas holidays. I told him about my idea for Homer and asked him if he would be the voice of Mr. Southwell. He agreed, and I knew he would be perfect.

Not only does Lewis have a funny, quick mind, he also has the Southern accent Homer needed to be believable. Lewis would make the perfect Homer.

I was going to do the spoof the afternoon of New Year's Eve.

I got to the station early to put the finishing touches on the show. About fifteen minutes before show time, my phone rang. It was Lewis. He told me that his soon-to-be ex-wife was flying to Mississippi to visit her family. She was changing planes in Atlanta, and she wanted Lewis to meet her at the Atlanta airport so they could fight. He felt obligated to go see her.

I said, "Well, Lewis, since she came all the way from Chicago to fight, I think the least you can do is go see her." He thanked me for understanding, and we hung up.

It suddenly occurred to me that I had no show put together as a backup. Not only that, because of the holiday, the radio station was empty. I walked back through the desolate station, hoping to find somebody ... anybody ... who could be my Homer Southwell. I went back into the sales department, and there sat one of our salesmen. He was late with his expense account and was trying to get it finished before the holiday.

I quickly explained that I was in trouble and needed him to play the part of Homer Southwell. After a little coaxing, he agreed.

I had made some flash cards with some of the lines I had written on them. The salesman was nervous, and I was nervous because he was nervous.

The "On Air" light came on, and I said a silent prayer: "Lord, get me through this and I'll quit smoking."

We went on the air, and it could not have gone better. My salesman friend turned into Homer Southwell right before my eyes.

The first caller was a man who said he was originally from Maine. In a very friendly voice, he said, "Mr. Southwell, I'm afraid I find your attitude disturbing."

Before he could say another word, Homer jumped right through the phone. He said, "I find your accent disturbing." Without giving the poor man a chance to say a word, he went on. "What the hell are you doing here anyway? Did you get tired of eating lobster and come South for a decent meal?"

After that call the telephones went absolutely crazy. We did that hour in full combat gear.

Toward the end of the hour, Homer said, "Before we sign off, I have a message I want to share with the radio audience." He went on in a very serious voice. "Do not allow your children to play with Yankee children. Teach your kids to make fun of them and to ridicule the way they talk. That way, they will not be happy here, and maybe they will put their parents under pressure to move back up north where they belong."

Homer closed by saying, "Please buy my book. Read it and take my advice. If you are from the North, get somebody to read it to you."

The fallout from the show was more than I had expected. People called the station and wrote letters for more than two weeks.

About a week after the show I received a call from Atlanta's (and perhaps the Southeast's) largest bookseller.

The lady said they had received hundreds of phone calls from people who wanted to buy Homer's books. She said, "Please promise me that the next time you're going to have an author in town who is that hot you'll call me so I can set up an autographing party for him."

You can't fool all the people all the time, but if you have your own radio show, you can come real close.

THE NERD

My friend Dan Fitzpatrick and I were co-hosting a show one Saturday afternoon.

Our topic was, "What is a nerd?" We were trying to find out all about nerds.

We asked, "How does a nerd dress? What kind of a job would a nerd have? Where would a nerd go to college? What kind of a car does a nerd drive? What does a nerd do for entertainment?"

We were having a great time, and the callers were into the spirit of the show and giving some very funny descriptions of a nerd.

About halfway through the show, a young man called and said, "Mr. Porch, my name is Robbie. I'm twelve years old, and I have a definition of a nerd." I knew he was serious. What I didn't know was that he was about to read me a definition out of his dictionary. I said, "Go ahead, pal. Tell me what is a nerd."

He took a deep breath and said, "Nerd: a noun. One who is uncool, a person who for one reason or another does not fit in with his peer group. Organ unknown."

I did not want to embarrass him, and I had intended to go right on to the next call. However, when he said, "Organ unknown," Dan fell on the floor, laughing like an absolute wild man. That was all it took. I went into gales of laughter. We did a commercial, came back and were still laughing. The more we thought about a nerd having an unknown organ, the more we laughed.

This happened many years ago, but until this day, whenever I hear somebody called a nerd, I wonder if he has an unknown organ.

PUNCH LINES

One of my favorite topics is "punch lines." The premise is a simple one. I tell my listeners to call and give me the punch line to their favorite joke. I think a good punch line will stand on its own.

When you hear a punch line, one of two things happens. It either reminds you of the joke it goes to, or, in your mind, you make up a joke to go with the punch line.

I have only one rule when I do punch lines: it must be clean. I don't care how filthy the joke is, as long as the punch line is clean.

Over the years we have elevated several punch lines to our "Punch Line Hall of Fame."

1. He'll bite you.
2. The one in the middle is definitely Willie Nelson.
3. Honest, officer, the midget was on fire when I got here.
4. Hey, lady! Your sign fell down!
5. What do you think this is — a duck?
6. Want a bite of my sandwich?
7. The first thing I'm going to do is get the brakes on this truck fixed.
8. Your monkey's on fire.
9. The regiment votes to repair it.
10. Paint my house.

See any of your favorites?

MATRICULATING

One day I wrote myself the following "Letter to Ludlow" and read it on the air:

Dear Ludlow,

I am outraged. I just found out that in the City of Atlanta school system, grades one through twelve, our children are being required to matriculate every day in school.

I am very upset. Please read this letter on the air and see if we can't get something done about this.

Angry in Atlanta

When I had finished reading the letter, I said in a very solemn voice, "What is this world coming to?"

The first caller said, "Why, Ludlow, all that means is —" Before he could finish, I cut him off and said, "Come on, now. We have to keep it clean. We can talk about this like adults."

I took several more calls. Some of them understood what I was doing and some didn't.

Then one of those dream calls came in. It was a man who said he was calling from just outside Montgomery, Alabama. I could tell by the serious tone of his voice that he had swallowed the bait.

He said, "Ludlow, did you go to school in the Atlanta area?"

I told him that I did. He said, "Were they doing that in school when you went?"

I said, "I'm not real proud of it, but I think they were probably doing more when I was in school than they're doing now."

He paused, took a deep breath, and said, "I went all through school in Montgomery, Alabama, and I will guarantee you one thing. If they were doing it there, they were doing it in the bathroom."

The more he talked about it, the more upset he became.

I finally said, "I don't want you to be too upset about this because survey after survey has shown that there is less matriculating going on at the University of Alabama than at any other major college in the United States."

That seemed to make him feel better.

Sometimes we all need to pause and think about who we issue driver's licenses to.

— from —

LEWIS & ME & SKIPPER MAKES 3 (1991)

AERO, MEDICO AND OTHER PHOBIAS

When I tell you that Skip was afraid to fly, what I really mean is that he was terrified to fly. I'm not sure exactly where this fear came from, but I know that for many years, there was no way to get him on an airplane. In today's business world, refusing to fly makes life very difficult.

I decided that if I could get four or five drinks into him, we could overcome his phobia. He was going somewhere or other to cover a football game, and I was able to persuade him that contrary to what the experts said, it was possible to find courage when you were arm and arm with Jack Daniels. My wife and I took him to the airport and got there early enough for a visit to the Crown Room. I made sure that his glass was full for ninety minutes, and he got braver and braver with every drink. By the time we got him to his gate, he was telling us about his secret ambition to be a wing walker and barnstorm the country.

The last thing he said was, "This is going to be a piece of cake. I'm going to volunteer for the Flying Tigers as soon as I get back." He disappeared down the tunnel, softly humming, "Off We Go, into the Wild Blue Yonder," and I felt like the world's greatest psychiatrist.

On the way home, we stopped for a nice, leisurely dinner. When we drove into our driveway a few hours later, there was Skip sitting on his suitcase waiting for us.

"How far did you get?" I asked.

"By the time I got to the first class section I was completely sober," he said, "and I knew that all the people around me were going to die in a fiery crash."

Once, when he was the sports editor for the *Chicago Sun Times*, he got a job offer from a newspaper in San Francisco. They wanted him to fly out for an interview. It was a great opportunity, so rather than fly, he took two weeks' vacation and rode a train all the way to San Francisco. He simply planned his life so that he never had to face the stark terror of getting on another airplane. He made a lot of jokes about it, but Skip's fear of flying was absolutely paralyzing.

In 1977, my mother died, and Skip was still living in Chicago. Someone called him and told him what had happened. I want you to know that he caught the next plane to Atlanta. Skip Grizzard is a hell of a guy.

Flying, however, is only one of the fears that Skip carries with him. One night we both wound up at what was billed as a seance. It was held in the private home of a friend of ours who believed in such things. There were ten or twelve people there, and our hostess had set up a nice bar in the kitchen.

When the seance started, we were told that the spirits would not come if there were any light except candlelight. So the electric lights were turned off, and four women sat down around a card table and held hands. With the candles flickering and our hostess speaking to the spirits, it looked like a scene out of an old Basil Rathbone movie. Except for the three candles burning in the living room, the whole apartment was dark, including the kitchen where the bar was set up.

"I want a drink," Skip whispered in my ear.

"The bar is in the kitchen," I said. "Help yourself."

"It's dark in there," he said.

"So take a candle with you."

"Will you go with me?"

I'm afraid I disturbed the approaching spirits with my outburst of laughter. I couldn't believe it. He was actually afraid to go into that dark kitchen alone. We never did contact any ghosts, but that was the biggest laugh I had had in years.

Skip is probably the only person in the history of medical science to make more money off his heart surgery than his doctor. He has made dozens of speeches about it and written hundreds of newspaper columns recounting his near meeting with St. Peter. He even wrote a book about it called *They Tore Out My Heart and Stomped That Sucker Flat.* In whatever medium, he has managed to find a lot of humor in what could easily have been his last time at bat.

He will tell anybody who will listen that the doctors and nurses at Emory University hospital saved his life, but that's now. He had a different attitude beforehand.

On the morning of his first surgery, I was alone with him in his room. His worst nightmare was about to come true. Someone he hardly knew was going to cut him with a knife, and he was not going to be able to hotfoot it out of the area. Like anybody, Skip was scared of death. I was making small talk, trying not to be morbid, when suddenly he reached up and took my hand. It was to me a very tender, moving moment. In a voice barely above a whisper he said, "Lud, you have to promise me something."

"Anything, anything," I said, practically sobbing.

He swallowed and said, "If I should die, kill the doctor."

There's a curious disease that nobody has ever found a cure for. It's called Black Cord Fever, and it afflicts males with a particular predisposition: those who are both a) drinking and b) afraid to be alone.

Lewis and Skip both suffered from Black Cord Fever. It is not a fatal disease, but it can be expensive. When you are infected, you pour yourself another drink, find the nearest telephone and call everybody you ever met in your life.

The first call is usually to a friend who is in your

local dialing area. As the evening wears on, however, you start in on the long distance calls. It is not uncommon for a man with a bad case of Black Cord Fever to call the long distance operator to get the phone number of an old Army buddy in Syracuse whose last name he just can't remember.

I hope someday Jerry Lewis or somebody will put on a telethon for the victims of Black Cord Fever. Others may not see it as so important, but I have great sympathy for those who suffer from this malady because of my relationship with Lewis and Skip, both of whom should be poster adults for Black Cord Fever.

Skip called me at home one night. I knew at once that he was with Jack Daniels. He had worked all day at the Atlanta paper and had gone straight to a watering hole. It was about eleven o'clock, and he was pretty far along.

"Skip, where are you?" I asked.

He said, "If I tell you, you'll want to come get me."

I finally convinced him I wanted to meet him for a drink. He liked that idea and said he was at the downtown Marriott Hotel. I told him I would meet him in the lobby and that, no matter what happened, he was not to leave. He said he couldn't leave because he didn't remember where he had left his car.

I dressed quickly and went straight to the hotel lobby. No Skip. I went into the bar. Still no Skip. I checked the restaurant; he was nowhere to be found.

I was about ready to give up and call it a night when I noticed a phone booth in the lobby with the door closed and the receiver cradle empty. I walked over and peered in, and there sat the Skipper on the phone booth floor talking to a college buddy that he had not spoken to in years. He was wearing slacks and a white dress shirt, but had no recollection of where his coat, tie or car was. He did, however, remember that we were going to have a drink together.

I convinced him to go home with me and we would try to find his car the next day. It took us all Saturday morning, but we finally found it in the parking lot of the old Mouse Trap Restaurant. We never did find his coat and tie.

Once, when Skip was living in Chicago, he called me. I knew the second I heard his voice that he had a bad case of Black Cord Fever. He was as homesick as any man could be; he was also very depressed. He and Fay were having problems, and she had moved out. He was so down that I was really worried about him. I tried to talk him into taking a few days off and flying home. He reminded me that he didn't fly. We talked for about an hour, and the longer we talked the more depressed he became. I finally said, "Skip, I'm coming after you." I hung up the phone and told my wife that we were driving to Chicago. If you don't know, Atlanta is about 45,000 miles from Chicago.

We got to the outskirts of the Windy City during their five o'clock rush. I stopped at a pay phone and called Skip for directions. He was so excited to hear a voice from home that he almost jumped through the phone. He gave me directions and said he would meet me at a certain intersection. I told him that the traffic was terrible, so he needed to allow me enough time to make it. We started into town in the worst traffic jam I had seen in years. When I was within a mile or so of our meeting spot, I saw Skip running down the center line of the four-lane street we were on. The traffic was just inching along, and he was looking in all the cars trying to find me.

When he finally got to our car, he laughed like a loon, and we must have hugged for ten minutes right there in the middle of the street. It was probably the finest reunion I was ever involved in.

Skip had made arrangements to go home with us for a few days, so we left Chicago and started south. It was during the C.B. radio craze, and Skip had watched carefully as I used the C.B. to get traffic and Smokey reports. We decided to drive all night so we could get Skip into the South before he absolutely busted a gut. I got sleepy, and Skip offered to drive while I caught a nap. We were cruising along about three in the morning, and as soon as I shut my eyes, Black Cord Fever hit Skip. He was lonely and just had to talk to somebody. There was the C.B. radio, and while he was not exactly sure how to use the thing, he just had to try. I was anxious to hear what he was going to say, so I didn't let on that I was still awake. He put the microphone to his mouth, and somewhere in the dark Indiana night I heard him say softly, "Hi there... my name is Skip Grizzard."

History does not tell us how many truckers laughed so hard they ran off the road.

Now that I think about it, it just may be that Skip's endless pursuit of women is not so much a result of his attraction to the opposite sex as of his fear of sleeping alone. In fact, on those evenings when he doesn't have the company of a lady friend, Skip sleeps with a black Lab named Catfish Smith. The dog was a gift from Vince Dooley and was named for the legendary University of Georgia football player.

Catfish is a loving, delightful dog who manages to stay in trouble most of the time.

The following is a partial list of the things Catfish ate during the first year of his life:

2 TV remote controls;

2 pairs of eyeglasses;

2 eyeglass cases;

1 coffee table;

3 bannister railings;

1 bannister;

1 complete set of patio furniture;

7 assorted dog bowls;

2 whole chickens;

1 bag of Reese's Peanut Butter Cups including all packaging;

1 leather wallet including Visa, MasterCard, and American Express cards;

1 sofa leg;

2 full-grown geese; and

1 set of car keys.

He was also the prime suspect in the disappearance

of numerous other missing objects, but the items listed above have been proven to be his responsibility.

Whenever Skip was home alone with Catfish, he was constantly going to the door to let the dog out. Catfish loved the outdoors, and when he wanted to go out, he would bark nonstop until Skip responded.

Skip got the idea that his life would be greatly improved if he had a doggie door installed for the exclusive use of Mr. Catfish. The door was accordingly installed, Skip was off the hook, and Catfish was delighted.

Skip had to make an overnight trip and decided to leave the doggie door open so his dog could come and go as he pleased. He put out plenty of food and water on the floor and departed on his journey.

He returned the next afternoon to find eleven dogs in his den. A large English Sheepdog was sound asleep on his sofa. There were dogs sleeping in chairs in front of his fireplace, and none of the visitors bothered to move or even wake up.

It was apparent that Catfish, like his master, did not like to sleep alone.

JUST A BOWL OF BUTTER BEANS

One of the things I love best about Skip Grizzard is that he is Southern to the marrow and proud of it. He also has certain Southern quirks, one of the funniest of which is his attitude toward food.

Skip is forty-five years old and, by his own admission, has never had a healthy meal in his life. He has been married and divorced three times. He has been engaged to all the eligible women in the seven southeastern states and certain parts of Florida. In his forty-five years, he has held over twenty jobs, traveled all over the world, and judged a goat milk-off in Abbeville, Louisiana. The only consistent thing in his life seems to be the Waffle House. It is his favorite restaurant in the whole world. He seems to feel a oneness with all Waffle House employees. He proudly proclaims that they are the only people in the world who can fix eggs "over medium well." I never heard of eggs "over medium well," but he is convinced that that is the only way Christian people should eat eggs.

He was having breakfast one morning at the Marriott Hotel in New Orleans. The waiter was named Keith. Skip ordered bacon, grits and two eggs "over medium well." Keith said nothing, but his eyebrows went up about two inches. He returned with the breakfast. Skip poked into the yellow part of his egg and said in a disgusted tone, "These eggs are not 'over medium well.' They are over, by God, raw!"

Keith straightened his little black bow tie and said, "I

will tell the chef, sir."

He removed Skip's breakfast and returned to the kitchen. When he came back a few minutes later, Skip took one look and said, "I wish to hell I was at the Waffle House. These eggs are not 'over medium well.'"

"Pardon me, sir," harrumphed Keith, "but could you describe exactly what 'over medium well' means?"

Skip took a deep breath and said, " 'Over medium well' means that the yellow is not running toward the edge of the plate. The yellow is crawling toward the edge of the plate."

"Crawling, sir?" asked Keith.

"You got it," confirmed Skip.

He took the plate and disappeared into the kitchen for the third time. When he returned, he said, "I hope these will be satisfactory, sir."

"The eggs are perfect," said Skip, "but everything else is cold."

It was at this point that Keith had what can only be described as a complete emotional breakdown. He buried his face in a napkin and started to cry. He ran from the table sobbing uncontrollably. Skip dipped his cold toast into his over medium well eggs and, with a puzzled look on his face, asked, "Reckon what's wrong with old Keith?"

Keith is only one in a long line of servers whose emotional well-being has been put in jeopardy by Skip. Skip decided early on that grits were some kind of health food. As a result, he adds either bacon or sausage grease, a large dob of cow butter, and loads of black pepper. Any healthful properties belonging to grits are more than made up for with these additions. He calls his concoction "Grits Grizzard," a dish that has been now outlawed by the health departments in three states.

Whenever possible, Skip tries to order only white food for breakfast. He orders his now-famous eggs "over medium well," grits and biscuits with sawmill gravy poured over them. It is entirely possible that one could go snow blind eating breakfast with Skip.

He thinks the four basic food groups are the Waffle House, Harold's, the Varsity and Sweat's Barbecue.

Once, while traveling in Europe, he was offered some squid. He declined, saying that he had once seen the movie *20,000 Leagues Under the Sea* and he would not eat anything Kirk Douglas could not kill.

Skip likes all Southern-style food. As a matter of fact, that is the only style of food he really loves. Once, while driving to the Gator Bowl in Jacksonville, we decided that we wanted a real Southern gourmet meal. We had been staying at Hilton Head Island for a week preceding the game, and while Hilton Head is in South Carolina and in the Deep South, the food in all the restaurants there is decidedly yankee.

We were going south on I-95 and stopped at a place called Kitty's Kountry Kitchen. I learned at my mother's knee that you should never eat in a place where the owner spells "Country" with a "K." Common sense will tell you that anybody who can't spell "Country" sure as heck can't read a cookbook. We looked at the menu and noticed that the first item said simply, "Chicken."

The waiter was a gentleman with a name tag that read "Earl."

"How is the chicken prepared?" asked Skip.

"It is smothered, sir," replied Earl.

"I don't care how you killed it," Skip declared. "What I want to know is, do you have any fried chicken?"

"Fried chicken is not good for you," Earl answered. "Too much grease."

"Earl," said Skip with a frown, "are you here to wait on tables or practice medicine?"

A quick check of the menu showed that there was nothing mashed, fried or starchy. So we left, unfed. We walked out into the parking lot, by this time starving to death. Across the street from Kitty's Kountry Kitchen was an old clapboard store. The hand-lettered sign out front said, "Walt's Texaco/Grocery Store/Notary."

Skip lit up like a carnival midway. "Come on," he said. "We're going to have a real Southern meal."

We walked across the road. There were double screen doors that said, "Colonial is Good Bread," in bright yellow and orange letters. There was a fist-sized ball of cotton fastened to the top of the screen. The inside of the store was dark even though the lights were on.

"Come in the house," said the old man behind the counter as we pulled open the screen door.

"How ya doin'?" we asked.

"Never been better and had less," he answered. "Can I hep ya?"

"We're going to have us a little dinner," Skip said.

"You pick it out, and I'll ring her up," said Walt.

Skip was absolutely beaming as we walked around the old store shopping. There was a bright red drink box against the wall. The yellow writing on it said, "Royal Crown Cola ... Best by Taste Test." We pulled two six-and-a-half-ounce Cokes out of the freezing cold, murky water. We then bought a box of soda crackers and a loaf of white bread. We continued to wander around and found the sardines, two Moon Pies, a box of Fig Newtons and some pork and beans. Skip hollered to Walt at the front of the store, "You got any baloney?"

"Was Eleanor Roosevelt ugly?" Walt hollered back. "You know I got baloney."

He escorted us back to the meat counter, where we ordered six slices of baloney. He cut them off with a knife. "Speck you gonna need some cheese, ain't ya?" he asked.

"We need about a hunk or a hunk and a half of cheese," Skip answered.

We bought paper plates, plastic spoons, and a 49-cent can opener. While we were paying Walt, I noticed two signs on the wall behind the old brass cash register. One said, "Jesus Loves You." The sign directly below it read, "Absolutely No Credit."

Walt bade us farewell by saying, "Y'all hurry back."

We pulled the car under the shade of a giant live oak tree and spread our South Georgia luau on the hood of the car. I don't know if it was my hunger or my Southern roots, but it was probably one of my top two or three all-time memorable meals.

When we had finished our last Fig Newton, we sat down in the grass to finish our Coke and savor the moment.

"Do you know what would really make this meal complete?" Skip asked between lazy draws on his Marlboro.

"What?"

"If we went back to Kitty's Kountry Kitchen and whipped old Earl's ass with that smothered chicken."

There have been many changes in both our lives since that long-ago meal. Wives, jobs and lifestyles have all changed. Our careers have consumed us so that we don't get to spend as much time together as we would like.

When we do get together, though, we often wind up talking about favorite times and favorite meals, and we never forget to mention the one catered by a gentleman named Walt.

Precious memories ... how they linger.

BEATING A DEAD HORSE IS MORE FUN THAN YOU THINK (1992)

SOUTHERN FACES

The Southern Belle

In the South, we have always been proud of our women. A quick survey by even a nearsighted person will prove what I have always known. Southern women are the most beautiful in the world. Stand on any street corner in the Deep South and you will find that about seventy percent of the Southern Belles you see are drop-dead beautiful, and the other thirty percent could win the Miss Ohio beauty contest by just showing up.

Over the decades, the beauty of Southern women has inspired songs, poems and novels. In the Old South, even a hint of an insult toward a young lady could result in a duel. Just the sound of their names conjures up images of beauty, charm and grace: Patsy Jean, Amber, Betty Jo and, of course, Scarlett.

However, it takes more than beauty, charm, grace and a name to make one a true Southern Belle. There is a strict — and I mean strict — code of conduct that every true Southern Belle adheres to. The code is not written down anywhere. It can only be learned at the knee of a Southern Belle mama. Once learned, however, the code is never violated. The penalty for violation is to be thought forward, brazen or brash, or, in the case of the most flagrant violation, to be deemed "common white trash."

Southern Belles have a long list of things that they never do. This list is not written down anywhere either, but is as much a part of their lives as "the vapors." Let's take a look at some of the things true Belles would never do.

Southern Belles never smoke on the street. There are no rules against smoking, but very strict rules about where they may smoke. It is perfectly all right to smoke in a restaurant as long as they are sitting down. They must never be seen standing or walking with a cigarette in their hand. When in public, they must never light their own cigarette. For a true Southern Belle, there will always be someone near at hand to take care of that small task.

A Southern Belle never goes into a bar or lounge without an escort. And once there, she never tries to impress her date by showing him how she can tie a knot in a cherry stem with her tongue.

A true Southern Belle would never, and I mean never, scold or speak harshly to a waiter or waitress. There are no exceptions. If a waitress should spill a pitcher of Salty Dogs in her lap, the true Belle will smile sweetly and say, "Let me help you clean that up, sugar." Never in her life will a Southern Belle be rude to someone acting in a service capacity. In a bar or restaurant, a true Southern Belle would no more speak loudly than she would order a vodka shooter. If word ever got out that she was drinking tequila, sucking a piece of lime and licking salt off the back of her hand, she would be thrown out of the Junior League before you could say "Montgomery, Alabama." And she would never drink anything out of a can — no place, no way, no how.

In a restaurant, the Southern Belle will always order the middle-priced item on the menu. If she orders the cheapest thing, she might leave the impression that she thinks her date can't afford to be there. If she orders the most expensive thing, he might think she is too extravagant. Once her dinner has arrived, she knows not to eat everything on her plate. Just like her mama told her, she will always leave something on the plate for Mr. Manners.

A Southern Belle would never call a man outside of her family on the phone. There are only three exceptions to this rule: a fireman, a policeman or her doctor — and even in these cases she would prefer that a woman answer.

She would rather die a slow, painful death than carry a white purse or wear white shoes before Easter or after Labor Day. She would never wear gloves without a hat.

When she gets on an airplane, she is dressed with the same formality that she would be dressed for her funeral.

When she gets married, she wears a white wedding dress. This rule holds even if she has been to bed with every member of the Atlanta Falcons and two guys she met at a Burger King drive-thru window.

She would never hurt anyone's feelings intentionally, but when angered, she can deliver a tongue-lashing that would bring the Devil himself to his knees.

A Southern Belle never sweats. It simply is not done. Nor does she whistle. The last time she tried was when she was six years old. Her mother told her, "A whistling girl and a crowing hen never come to no good end." She never whistled again.

She would never talk about another man with the man she is with. She would never eat a raw weenie in public. She would never spit, request a Jerry Lee Lewis record be played at her wedding reception, or put sugar in her cornbread.

She would never date a man named Three-Fingered

Jerome, sit spraddle-legged, or take lasagna to a church covered-dish supper.

She is a delight, a wonder and a mystery, but most importantly she's ours.

You're in a Heap of Trouble, Boy

Southern policemen are a wonderful part of every Southerner's life. They are a breed unto themselves. They are not only keepers of the peace; they are our friends and neighbors, and they are the butt of many of our jokes.

Some of the most interesting characters I have ever known have worn a badge. There was a policeman in my youth who was a legend to me and my peers. I will simply call him Buster.

He was small for a Southern cop, about 5'6" tall, and weighed about 140 pounds. What he lacked in size, however, he made up in pure rattlesnake meanness. It was said that Buster would fight a circle saw and spot it the first two licks. His claim to fame, however, was not his size or his meanness; it was his prowess with a blackjack.

The story was that one dark night, a group of the local good old boys were having a crap game in the living room of one of their homes. They were so into the rolling of the bones that they didn't even notice Buster walk quietly into the room. In a quiet voice, Buster said, "Y'all lay down on the floor. I'm fixin' to take this whole lash-up to jail for runnin' a crap game." Everybody complied, except for one old boy who jumped through an open window. Buster was right behind him. The crap shooter was more fleet of foot than little Buster, though, and it soon became apparent to our hero that he was losing ground.

When about half a city block separated them, Buster

pulled out his blackjack and threw it like a tomahawk. Witnesses said later that it hit the man in the back of the head and he fell like he had been pole-axed.

Later, knowing of Buster's violent leanings, someone jokingly asked him why he had not shot the suspect. Buster said, "Aw, he's a good old boy—besides, I know his daddy."

A city policeman in a small west Georgia town was standing in the middle of the street directing traffic. Right behind him was a larger-than-life-sized statue of a Southern general. A carload of northern tourists stopped for the red light, and, pointing to the statue, the driver asked the officer, "Whose statue is that?"

Without missing a beat, the policeman said, "It's ours."

In a small Tennessee town, the local smokey stopped a car carrying four black men. He waddled up to the car and said, "Where are you fellas from?"

"Chicago," said the driver.

"Oh yeah?" the officer snarled. "If you all are from Chicago, how come you got them Illinois plates on your car?"

In the small town of Abbeville, Louisiana, a burglar alarm sounded in the middle of the night at a warehouse. Two of Abbeville's finest responded. They slid into the parking lot, blue lights flashing and siren screaming. Pistols drawn, one went around the left side of the warehouse and the other went around the right side. They met in back and shot each other.

Buford and Leon, two middle Georgia policemen, stopped a yankee tourist for speeding. The man was very loud and belligerent and insisted the posted speed limit was not 55 mph, but 80. To prove his point, he showed them the sign with that figure on it. Leon said, "That ain't the speed limit; that's the highway number." They gave him a ticket, and as they were walking back to their car, the tourist heard Leon say to Buford, "I'm shore glad we stopped him before he got to 441."

The most typical Southern cop I ever knew or heard about was my boyhood friend "Fats" Funderburk. His real name, or course, was not "Fats," but since he weighed about 240 pounds when we were in the seventh grade, "Fats" was all he had ever been called. I had not seen or heard from him in about twenty years, but through the grapevine, I had heard that he was a captain on a suburban Atlanta police force.

My cousin Doodle was a mechanic and part-time race-car driver. He was also the proud owner of a souped-up Corvette. He needed to borrow my larger four-door car to pick up some visitors at the airport, so I went to his house to exchange cars. Doodle is a very hospitable man, and while I was at his house, he held a gun on me and insisted that I have two drinks before I left.

When it was time to go, he went outside with me to

show me how to drive his "faster than lightning" Corvette. When I cranked it up, I had never heard such power; even idling, it sounded like it could go 200 hundred miles an hour in "Park." It was by far the most powerful machine I had ever been around. I didn't mind because the two drinks had made me relaxed and confident that I could handle anything.

Driving home, I had on the radio and both windows open. It happened just as I got on the entrance ramp to the expressway. The wind was in my face and Hank Williams on the radio was singing, "If you got the money, Honey, I got the time." Suddenly, without warning, I became sixteen years old again. I started to sing along with old Hank as I mashed the accelerator down, down, down. When the entrance ramp dumped me into the expressway, I was doing about 80 and still singing along with old Hank.

I was just getting to the part about "We'll go honky-tonking, and we're going to have a time" when I noticed the blue lights flashing in my rearview mirror. My first thought was "Oh hell! Here I am, whiskey on my breath, speeding, and every blue light in the world going round and round behind me." I pulled over and the blue lights pulled up right behind me. I was looking into my rearview mirror, trying to think up the world's biggest lie, when I saw my boyhood friend "Fats" Funderburk pry himself out of the police car. Even in semi-darkness he was easy to recognize. He had that same unmistakable waddle that he had in the seventh grade. I almost jumped with joy. There was no way that my beloved "Fats" was going to give me a ticket. Why, we had been such good friends that if I had asked, he would have fixed a murder rap for me. I was so happy about my good luck that I decided to have a little fun with my long-lost chum.

I left the motor running because I knew that would irritate him. He was carrying one of those great big old flashlights — the kind with about fifteen batteries. It was the multi-use variety: you could use it to light your way or to hit a suspect upside the head.

He stopped beside my open window but did not bend over to make eye contact. He said, "Let me see your drime liam." I pretended to look for my license while that powerful motor idled louder and louder. I knew it was getting his goat when he started to slap that huge flashlight into his open palm.

"Do you know how fast you was going, Boy?" he asked.

"No, I was down in the engine room at the time," I answered.

"Don't get smart with me, Boy."

"The trouble with you cops," I suggested, "is that you're out here harassing decent citizens when you got lawbreakers double-parked all over town."

"Decent citizens, my ass," he said, still trying to control his voice. "You wuz doin' damn near a hundred mile an hour."

When I was sure that he was about to drag me through the open window, I handed him my license. He saw my name at once and for the first time bent over far enough to look me in the face. He smiled a big toothy grin and said, "You sumbitch … where you been?" I got out of the car, and we hugged and shook hands and had a reunion right there on the side of the expressway.

He said, "I just busted a bootlegger, and my patrol car has about two gallons of that old see-through liquor in the trunk. Why don't we have us a little drink?"

The South is full of wonderfully colorful characters — none more colorful than our policemen.

Fortune-Tellers

We Southerners are a superstitious crowd. We believe in everything from wart witches to haints. (A haint is a Southern ghost.) We believe that if you step on a crack, your mama is a "goner." We believe that kerosene, when used properly, can cure most of mankind's ills. We believe that a homemade mustard plaster is more effective than open-heart surgery.

We know, for an absolute scientific fact, that cats are bad luck, buckeyes are good luck, and that if you break a mirror your life will not be worth living for seven years.

We are also the home office for fortune-tellers nationwide. Any Southerner worth his grits can tell you how to find a fortune-teller who truly has "the gift." If you need to find one, here's how to go about it:

The first thing you look for is a sign; there are two types. One type has the outline of an Indian head complete with war bonnet. It reads "Madame Zelda" or "Sister Marie — Indian Advisor and Healer." The other type has the outline of a hand. It reads "Madame Zelda" or "Sister Marie — Palmist and Reader: Knows All, Sees All and Tells All." Parked close to the sign is a house trailer. I never figured out why, if they knew all and saw all, they had to live in a house trailer. The inside of the trailer is decorated in Early Tacky. It looks like all the furnishings have been won at a county fair.

The fortune-teller always wears very bright clothes and a shawl. Real fortune-tellers will own two or three Chihuahua dogs with runny eyes. Everything in the trailer has red ball fringe — the sofa, the chairs, her shawl, and even the Chihuahua.

All fortune-tellers are female, and they are all married to gravy-sucking pigs who are too sorry to work. The husband's main function in life seems to be to help his wife hold one of those little, runny-eyed, yappin' dogs. He is always tall and skinny and reminds you of Henry Fonda in *The Grapes of Wrath*.

The cost of the actual reading is only the beginning of your expense. She will always have an extra cost for the product she wants to sell you.

If you are having problems with your love life, she will sell you a love potion that will make the object of your affection want to cut your lawn, defrost your refrigerator, and kiss you on the mouth.

If you have an enemy, she will sell you a matchbox full of cemetery dirt. All you have to do is sprinkle the dirt on your enemy's property and the wrath of God will descend on that person.

If you find yourself in need of money, she will have charms available that will make you rich beyond your wildest dreams.

In the course of your reading, your friendly neighborhood fortune-teller will tell you how she happened to be blessed with these wonderful powers: she is the seventh daughter of a seventh daughter. She was born with a veil over her face, and she is always one-quarter Cherokee Indian. She was put on this earth to help others, and she will always do whatever she can — except give you a free reading.

New Southerners

I guess I was about twelve years old before I met someone from the North. A new family moved into my neighborhood with a son about my age named Billy. I liked him at once. It was fun to listen to him talk. I had never known anyone who pronounced his "G's."

In school, he was teased a lot. It hurt his feelings, and, because he was my friend, it hurt me, too. Now, I'm the first to admit that it's hard not to laugh at someone who thinks gravy is a sauce and a ham biscuit is a little sandwich. Being Southern, however, my mama taught me that it was bad manners to make fun of people, and even worse to laugh out loud at them. In my beloved South, the worst thing that can be said about a person is that he is ill mannered.

Since the South has become a mecca for people raised in the North, it is important that we not ridicule, but rather attempt to educate them. In an effort to be politically sensitive, I have even stopped calling yankees yankees. I have coined the term New Southerners. It seems less harsh and does not conjure up memories of the War Between the States. I have put a list together of rules that will help our New Southerners hide the fact that "they ain't from around here."

We don't care how they did it in Cleveland, Detroit or Newark. If you really want to tick off a card-carrying, gravy-dipping son of these red clay hills, just tell him how much better things are done in the North.

Do not talk loud in a restaurant. This advice is particularly good for New Southern women. For some strange reason, they seem to think that everyone in the restaurant should be privy to their conversation. The rule of thumb is that only the people at your table should be able to hear you. If you are unable to speak that softly, then you should just hush.

All tissue is Kleenex, even if you prefer another brand name. Your conversation with the clerk should go like this: "I'd like a box of Kleenex." The Southern clerk will say, "What kind of Kleenex would you like?" Then and only then do you give him the brand name of your choice. You should also bear in mind that all refrigerators are Frigidaire, all copy machines are Xerox, and all sneakers are tennis shoes.

Never make any comment, pro or con, about grits. If you like 'em, eat 'em. If you don't, leave 'em alone. To try and tell a Southerner about grits is a perfect example of preachin' to the choir.

Never try to point out or explain about snow clouds. We don't understand or care about them. If you miss them, go where they are.

Never eat fried chicken with a knife and fork. If you do, the people around you will know three things:

a. You ain't from around here.
b. You are trying to be uppity.
c. You don't know nothin' about eating fried chicken.

Never go to a restaurant and order blood pudding, lamb or tongue sandwich. In the first place, they're not going to have it. In the second place, they're not going to know what you are talking about, and in the third place, nobody wants a waitress named Flonella laughing so hard she spills your water.

Never blow your car horn. It is much better to be killed in a fiery crash than to be a bad reflection on your family. Horn blowing in the South is considered rude — anytime … anyplace … and under any circumstances.

Never go out in the snow. Stay home and play with your kids. The rule of thumb in the South is that any snow of one inch or more constitutes a legal holiday.

There are three meals a day: breakfast, dinner, and supper. If you want lunch, the closest place to get it is Maryland.

Never refer to the War Between the States as the Civil War. In the South, General Sherman taught us that there was nothing civil about that war.

Never talk about gun control. Put it in the category with politics and religion and leave it out of polite conversation. Remember, New York City has very strict gun control laws.

Try not to be abrupt; try to soften what you say. Sprinkle your conversation with "please" and "thank-you." Never walk up to a box office and say "TWO!" Say, "May I have two tickets, please?"

When forced to send food back in a restaurant, try to make it sound like it was your fault. Never say, "This steak is raw!" Say, "Ma'am, I know I'm peculiar about my steaks, but if you'd ask that old boy in the kitchen to throw this back on the fire for a minute, I'd dance at your wedding." This way nobody is mad and you get your steak the way you like it.

Never accuse a Southerner of still fighting the War Between the States. It did not turn out so well the first time and no Southerner I know wants to try again.

I guess what all of these suggestions are meant to do is to tell you not to call attention to yourself. The average Southern child is taught from birth never to do anything to call attention.

Above all, remember that if you act like somebody, folks will treat you like you're somebody.

WE'RE ALL IN THIS ALONE
(1994)

SENTIMENTAL JOURNEYS

Co-Cola

It has become popular in the last few years to refer to everything as America's own, like "America's Team," "America's Truck" and "America's Network."

I have had a love affair all my life with America's soft drink, Coca-Cola (pronounced in the Deep South as Co-Cola). It was as much a part of my youth as red clay, marbles or Dagwood Bumstead.

When I was five or six years old, Coca-Cola was the ultimate treat; six ounces of heaven for only a nickel. It came in a bottle shaped a little like an hourglass. When you reached down into the murky, ice-cold water of Johnny Durham's drink box, you could always find the Coke by that wonderful bottle's shape.

There were other soft drinks on the market, and

most all of them gave you more for a nickel than did my beloved Coke. I must confess that several times on a real hot, humid Georgia day, I would find myself in a backsliding condition and go for the bigger size of a Pepsi or an R.C. I might even go for a Red Rock Cola or a Red Rock Ginger Ale. If my taste called for a fruit flavor, I would get an Orange Crush or a grape NeHi or even a strawberry-flavored Town Hall. These experiments were short-lived, I'm proud to say, because I always came back to "the pause that refreshes."

When World War II came along, Coke was one of the first things to become in short supply. In my six-year-old mind, I couldn't figure out how our soldiers and sailors were using Coca-Cola to whip the Germans and the Japanese. When I asked a grown-up, he said the army needed the sugar. That didn't make any sense to me, but I guess it was true because we won the war and got our Cokes back.

In my teen years, Coke became an even bigger part of my life. I'm not sure at what age a boy's hormones kick in and his mind turns from baseball, basketball and football to girls, and girls, and girls. I'm not sure when it happens, but I do remember all the signs of the ballistic hormones. There are ten sure signs:

1. You stop going barefooted.
2. Your haircut is suddenly important.
3. You shine your shoes without being told.
4. You try aftershave lotion even if you don't shave.
5. For the first time in your life, the telephone becomes important.

6. Your mother can never iron your shirt just right.
7. It is out of the question to wear a patch on your jeans.
8. You stop spitting.
9. You experiment to see if indeed "a little dab will do you."
10. You worry a lot about how tall you are.

It is at about this time when you introduce some new lines into your speech: "What are you doing after school?" "Want to stop by Glover's Pharmacy for a cherry Coke?" "Come on, I'll buy you a Coke."

I wonder how many teenage romances started out over a fountain Coke. The setting was not always the same, but from border to border and coast to coast, it looked something very much like this:

A teenage boy and girl sit at a soda fountain. The table is simulated marble; the chairs are wrought iron. On the table are two small fountain Cokes with a single paper straw in each glass. A ceiling fan spins slowly and silently overhead. Behind the counter stands the soda jerk wearing a starched Ike jacket, a white apron, and sometimes a black bow tie. All that atmosphere and it only costs a dime.

In addition to the flowering of young romance over two small Cokes, our teen years are filled with Coca-Cola. Shake a Coke with your thumb over the top and spray somebody. This is an all-purpose celebration or an all-purpose prank which can lead to a great deal of laughter or a punch in the mouth, depending on the sense of humor of the sprayee.

The ultimate snack is a handful of peanuts poured right into your bottle of Coke. It's tasty enough to make your eyes roll back in your head.

A Coke dessert? How about a scoop of vanilla ice cream into a big glass of that heavenly liquid; easy to make and fun to eat. It's called a Coke float.

Did you ever make Coca-Cola ice cream? It ain't peach, but it's wonderful.

Whenever I hear about cola wars, I have to smile. Coke not only tastes best, but it is so entwined with our country's history that it will always be number one by a mile.

When Henry Ford was still running a bicycle shop, Americans were enjoying Coca-Cola. When the dough-boys came home from the trenches of France, they wanted hamburgers and Cokes. Ask any World War II veteran how much he missed Coke. Co-Cola is as American as the flag.

My beautiful wife, Diane, summed it up best when she took a drink of Coke and said, "The taste of Coke is like the smell of bacon frying."

Gone but Not Forgotten

Time is a magician. I say that because time, for no good reason, can make things disappear. Sometimes they disappear almost overnight, like the Edsel; other things take years to vanish, like pocket watches.

That was the way it was with telephone booths. It seems like only yesterday phone booths were like a little home away from home. They were equipped with folding doors that closed to keep noise out and your secret conversation in. There was a small fan with rubber blades to keep you cool and a small seat so you could be comfy while you chatted away. The cost for all this luxury was five cents per call. Cool, comfortable, private, and it only cost a nickel!

You can say what you will about kryptonite being Superman's worst enemy, but take away that old-fashioned phone booth, and all that's left of the man of steel is a funny-looking guy in a suit and horn-rimmed glasses, looking for a place to change clothes.

When did women stop wearing hats and gloves? It seems to me that only yesterday, when you went downtown or to church or rode on an airplane, all of the women wore hats and gloves. Who decided that was no longer the thing to do?

What happened to those wonderful caps that nurses wore? They not only looked sharp, they were a badge of education, honor, dedication, and a silent pledge to fight human suffering wherever they found it. I wonder how many little girls decided to dedicate their lives to nursing because those caps were so striking. Who decided to throw them all away?

I wonder who the hero was who decided we didn't need vent windows in our cars anymore. I betcha he was the same yahoo who decided you didn't need a spare tire, because you could get by with an oversized doughnut in your trunk. Could he have been the one who got rid of the rumble seat and the running boards, and moved the dimmer switch off of the floorboard? I don't know who he was, but a good caning seems to be in order if we ever find out.

What happened to gas station attendants? It was a great comfort to pull up to a gas pump, run over that rubber hose, hear the bell ring, and just sit there. In about fifteen seconds, Marvin would come out of one of the bays (you knew his name was Marvin because it was sewn over his pocket). He was always wiping his hands off on a rag. His greeting was the same to every customer, "Can I hep you?"

Whatever happened to him? God, how I loved old Marvin. It wouldn't be so bad, except that Marvin has been replaced by an unsmiling guy with no name on his shirt. Mr. No Name sits inside a glass cage. He speaks to you in fractured English through an intercom that is carefully programmed to pick up every fourth word. The worst part is Mr. No Name doesn't even have the simple human decency to wipe his hands on a rag. No sense of tradition whatsoever. Goodbye Marvin; America misses you.

Whatever happened to *The Saturday Evening Post*? I

miss "Hazel," "The Perfect Squelch" and those wonderful Norman Rockwell covers.

I miss the old steam whistles on trains. The whistles on the diesel engines sound like an angry rhino passing gas.

I miss playing in old, abandoned sawdust piles (they don't allow grown-ups to do that).

I miss hide-and-seek (something else grown-ups can't do).

I miss Bing Crosby at Christmas time.

Sometimes it seems like I am a stranger on my own planet, or perhaps I'm not on my own planet. The one I came from had Roosevelt, Truman and Ike. It had penny loafers, poodle skirts, and John Wayne. It had kitchen matches, Henry J. automobiles, and the Brooklyn Dodgers.

Common sense tells me that, in the end, the calendar will always win, and in my heart I know that we live in a better world — a world without polio, Hitler or the black plague. Yes sir, all things considered, it is a better world, but I'm still a little worried about old Marvin.

Prison Movies, or "This Cracker Box Can't Hold Rocky"

Movies seem to go in cycles. In the 1930s and 1940s, Hollywood was turning out an average of two motion pictures a day. Love stories, Westerns, musicals and one of my favorites, the prison movie.

If anybody has made a good, old-fashioned prison movie in the last few decades, I don't know about it. I had great hopes for *Cool Hand Luke.* It turned out not to be a prison movie at all. It was a chain gang movie. Prison movies are filmed almost entirely indoors, and chain gang movies are filmed almost entirely outdoors. Chain gang movies are always set in the South with a lot of swamps for the inmates to work in. They have sadistic guards named Floyd or Rufus to abuse the convicts. Prison movies are usually set up north and the guards are all named Slade or Kincaid.

The jury is still out on why Hollywood no longer makes prison movies. I think there is a market for them. The formula is simple enough. You do exactly what movie makers did in the 1940s and 1950s.

The warden can be a good guy or a bad guy. If he is a good guy, he can be played by Pat O'Brien. If he is a bad guy, he can be played by Barton McLain.

The hero/convict can be a good guy who got framed or a louse who deserves everything he gets. If he is a good guy who got framed, he can be played by Joel McRae or Douglas Fairbanks, Jr. If he is a louse who deserves everything he gets, he can be played by James

Cagney, Edward G. Robinson or George Raft.

If he is a good guy who got framed, his name must be Steve. If he is a louse who deserves everything he gets, his name must be Rocky.

His girlfriend must be played by Sylvia Sydney or Clair Trevor. If Steve escapes from prison, it must be in order to prove his innocence. On the other hand, if Rocky (the louse) escapes, it is to resume his life of crime and to beat up Clair Trevor or Sylvia Sydney on occasion.

Any self-respecting prison movie must have at least one scene showing a convict being led to the electric chair by two guards, the warden and a priest. The priest has to be reading the Bible as they walk toward the chair. I have done extensive research and determined that no Protestants were ever executed in a prison movie.

When the louse is led out of his cell and starts his slow walk to the chair, several things must be happening:

• The priest must be looking at his Bible and muttering in a low voice with an Irish accent.

• The hallway leading to the chair must be lit by a series of forty-watt bulbs.

• One of the men on death row must be black, have a bass voice, and be singing "Swing Low Sweet Chariot." It is of paramount importance that he be a bass. (A tenor would probably invoke laughter from the priest and ruin the somber mood.)

• The louse must shake hands with the priest and say, "So long, Fodder." In the better prison movies, all condemned men are from New York City.

• Executions should only take place on stormy nights.
• The prison lights should dim so the audience will know that justice has been served, and the black guy can stop singing, and the priest can stop muttering.

I don't guess they will ever make another real prison movie, but if they do, I'm available as director and technical advisor.

Love

I think the most misunderstood thing in the world is love. Love is different for everybody. Poets and songwriters have been trying for years without success to tell us what love is and how it works. One songwriter put pen to paper and came up with "You always hurt the one you love." That's dumb on the face of it. Sometimes you hurt folks you don't give a rip about.

It all boils down to one simple fact: love means different things to different people.

Love is sitting up all night in a hospital waiting room.

Love is watching her sleep.

Love is the feeling you get watching your son get his first haircut.

Love is bringing her flowers when it's not a special occasion.

Love is when you enjoy her beating you at Scrabble.

Love is when she fixes your favorite meal and she is as tired as you are.

Love is the smell of baby powder.

Love is when she walks by your chair and touches the top of your head.

Love is the thing that makes you hum.

Love is the basis of religion, patriotism and all success. Love is the only thing that can make you deliriously happy and miserably sad at the same time.

Love does not mean never having to say you're sorry.

Love means being able to say you're sorry and really, really mean it.

Love is simply the most important thing in the world.